IN GOD'S IMAGE

IN GOD'S IMAGE

For Teenagers and New Believers

Shirley P. Soon

ELM HILL

A Division of
HarperCollins Christian Publishing

www.elmhillbooks.com

In GOD's Image
For Teenagers and New Believers

Published in Nashville, Tennessee, by Elm Hill, an imprint of Thomas Nelson. Elm Hill and Thomas Nelson are registered trademarks of HarperCollins Christian Publishing, Inc.

Hill titles may be purchased in bulk for educational, business, fund-raising, or sales promotional use. For information, please e-mail SpecialMarkets@ThomasNelson.com.

All Scripture quotations, unless otherwise indicated, are taken from the Holy Bible, New International Version®, NIV®. Copyright © 1973, 1978, 1984, 2011 by Biblica, Inc.® Used by permission of Zondervan. All rights reserved worldwide. www.Zondervan. com. The "NIV" and "New International Version" are trademarks registered in the United States Patent and Trademark Office by Biblica, Inc.®

Library of Congress Cataloging-in-Publication Data

Library of Congress Control Number: 2019933466

ISBN 978-1-400325450 (Paperback)
ISBN 978-1-400325467 (Hardbound)
ISBN 978-1-400325474 (eBook)

This book is dedicated to the Holy Spirit, the author's mentor.

Praise for
In GOD's Image

Understanding the Gospel of the Holy Bible can be difficult for some readers. There are so many concepts that it can be overwhelming to grasp them all. Luckily, *In GOD's Image* by Shirley P. Soon makes this process easier.

When I picked up this title, I wasn't sure what to expect. Books in this genre can be pushy when it comes to religious views, but I did not get that feeling while reading this one.

Each concept that the author wanted readers to understand has a dedicated chapter; occasionally, a chapter will use the same concept that was already introduced earlier in the book to explain another concept.

I liked that the author referenced her writings to the Bible, and strongly recommended that readers use their own Bible to follow along and read the verses for themselves.

The reference section at the end was full of information as well. All the works that the author cited are written by scholars and authors who know the Bible. I also learned that the author…taught a Sunday School and was a church librarian, which I felt helped give her work credibility.

Even though I know about the Gospel, I felt that I gained more knowledge and understanding about it from reading this book. Shirley P. Soon says that it is intended for teenage readers and new believers, and I believe that this is an accurate statement. However, I do believe that even those who are interested in the Gospel or want to discover a new religion would be able to understand the concepts that the author presents. Honestly, I recommend it to anyone who wants to learn more about Jesus Christ and the Gospel.

> — Katie Canedy, excerpted from an
> official OnlineBookClub.org review

In GOD's Image by Shirley P. Soon is a Christian non-fiction book that teaches new Christian believers and teenagers the fundamental principles of the Gospel. The writer›s tone is pleasant, simple, and didactic, while the book is filled with references to Biblical verses.

The author begins her book by discussing man's separation from God due to sin. She explains that because Adam and Eve disobeyed God in the Garden of Eden, sin entered the human race, which is why sin exists in a person's bloodline. However, by God's grace, people can be forgiven if they believe in Jesus and repent from their sins. Also, the writer signifies the importance of baptism, which symbolizes a believer's death to sin and resurrection to a new life in Christ. Next, the author explores the character of God, focusing specifically on the idea of the Trinity. She emphasizes that God is one, but he has three distinct persons, using Bible verses to clarify her position. Moreover, the author talks about the role of the Holy Spirit in a believer's life, focusing on the Holy Spirit's work of sanctification. With the Holy Spirit, a person is changed and begins displaying the attributes of God in his/her life.

This book contained several positive attributes, which made it thoroughly enjoyable. To be more precise, the text was unique and authentic, as the writer's ideas and opinions were original, thereby clearly showing that this book is a product of her own hard work. Furthermore, this book was expertly structured because the chapters were coherently linked to each other. What I liked most about the text was that it was persuasive and argumentative, as the author used evidence from numerous sources and facts from the Bible to justify her opinions.

This book will likely be preferred by readers who have recently become Christians. Also, Christians who want to increase their knowledge of the Gospel to be more effective witnesses will find the text useful.

—Nicholas Farmakis, excerpted from an official OnlineBookClub.org review

(Note: In this book, *GOD* will refer to the entire Trinity, while *God* will be used to refer to any and each of the persons in the Trinity (or Tri-Unity).)

TABLE OF CONTENTS

SECTION 1

THE GOSPEL

Our Mandate as Christians

Learning obedience through GOD's Word, the Bible, is our mandate as new, young Christians. To glorify GOD is our purpose! Everything we do should be an act of obedience to our GOD and Saviour, the Lord Jesus Christ. All of our actions should show our trust in the One who sacrificially gave His life for each of us, on the Cross.

> *I am the vine; you are the branches. If you remain in me and I in you, you will bear much fruit; apart from me you can do nothing...This is to my Father's glory, that you bear much fruit, showing yourselves to be my disciples.*
> —John 15:5, 8

To GOD be all glory!

I praise you because I am fearfully and wonderfully made; your works are wonderful...
> —Psalm 139:14

The world may define a sinner as someone who breaks man's law, doing something that might earn jail time. But that is not the true definition of a sinner in GOD's eyes. A true sinner is one who does not believe in GOD, and doesn't believe what GOD says in His Word. We are all sinners when we live our lives separate from GOD and oblivious to His loving sacrifice of His Son on the cross. To be free of sin is to acknowledge and accept GOD's gift.

To prepare us for His plan for reunification with mankind, GOD started inspiring men over many years to record His Word, the sixty-six books of the Holy Bible as we know it today. In the early days after mankind's creation, GOD spoke directly to His prophets, but today He speaks to us through His Word and also in the hearts of those who believe in Him, those who are sealed by His Holy Spirit.

Here are a few verses that speak of these truths:

In the beginning was the Word, and the Word was with God, and the Word was God.

—John 1:1

Beyond all question, the mystery from which true godliness springs is great:

He appeared in the flesh,
was vindicated by the Spirit,
was seen by angels,
was preached among the nations,
was believed on in the world, was taken up in glory.

—1 Timothy 3:16

GOD tells us that His Word was actually manifest in the flesh, and that happened for a very good reason! The very first man and woman broke GOD's very first law, and GOD had stipulated that if that first law was broken, there would be a penalty or consequence. Death was that penalty! The penalty of death was imprinted upon the very being of that couple—though the Bible doesn't state the exact method of this imprinting, given what we know now about genetics, it's not unreasonable to assume that it's in our very DNA. And all of their descendants would inherit this new aspect of mankind. All of their descendants were born with this new aspect of their DNA. So, it follows that we are all born sinners in the eyes of GOD!

The Word, Jesus, is the one and only Son of GOD. As a man and a woman can bring forth a child, so GOD, a spiritual being, brought forth a spiritual Son. The Son of GOD was brought into the world to get mankind out of their fix, after mankind broke GOD's Law and incurred that death penalty!

GOD used a godly woman to enable His Son to be born as a human in the world. This Son, Jesus, was one hundred percent sinless, yet because He was in the flesh, He was also one hundred percent human. Because of His sinless state, He could qualify to pay for the sins of all mankind. As Adam and Eve had broken that first law, incurring death; so one sinless Man, Jesus, could pay for that broken law, and could, through His death on the cross, release all people finally from death (Romans 5:14, 1 Corinthians 15:22).

So why would GOD do that? He sacrificed His Son because of His great love for His creation, mankind! But GOD still respected His creation enough to let man retain his power of choice, which had been given to mankind at mankind's creation.

So each man, woman, and child must make a personal choice to accept that Jesus died for him or her individually, before the death penalty is considered to have been paid on his or her behalf. That means you have to accept Christ's sacrifice, you yourself. No one can do that except you!

So how do you do that? You pray to GOD! Find a quiet place, and say your words to GOD out loud, directing them upwards. GOD will hear you! Guaranteed!

You might say, "GOD, I accept that your Son, Jesus, died on the cross for all my sins—past, present, and future. Forgive me for all those sins. I want to have a relationship with You, to obey You, and to love You! Amen!"

Do read the following chapters in this book to *find out more.*

CHAPTER 1

IT STARTED WITH
DISOBEDIENCE

When did it all start, this story of GOD and mankind?

It started with GOD's first law, after His creation of mankind.

> *The LORD God took the man and put him in the Garden of Eden to work it and take care of it. And the LORD God commanded the man, "You are free to eat from any tree in the garden; but you must not eat from the tree of the knowledge of good and evil, for when you eat from it you will certainly die."*
> —Genesis 2:15-17

Then GOD's first law was broken by the first man and woman.

> *Now the serpent was more crafty than any of the wild animals the LORD God had made. He said to*

the woman, "Did God really say, 'You must not eat from any tree in the garden'?"

The woman said to the serpent, "We may eat fruit from the trees in the garden, but God did say, 'You must not eat fruit from the tree that is in the middle of the garden, and you must not touch it, or you will die.'"

"You will not certainly die," the serpent said to the woman. "For God knows that when you eat from it your eyes will be opened, and you will be like God, knowing good and evil."

When the woman saw that the fruit of the tree was good for food and pleasing to the eye, and also desirable for gaining wisdom, she took some and ate it. She also gave some to her husband, who was with her, and he ate it. Then the eyes of both of them were opened, and they realized they were naked; so they sewed fig leaves together and made coverings for themselves.

—Genesis 3:1-7

After this, God declared punishment for the man and the woman's law-breaking. Here is how that punishment was declared:

1. The serpent was cursed.

So the LORD God said to the serpent, "Because you have done this, Cursed are you above all livestock and all wild animals! You will crawl on your belly and you will eat dust all the days of your life. And

I will put enmity between you and the woman, and between your offspring and hers; he will crush your head, and you will strike his heel."

—Genesis 3:14-15

2. The woman was cursed.

To the woman he said, "I will make your pains in childbearing very severe; with painful labor you will give birth to children. Your desire will be for your husband, and he will rule over you."

—Genesis 3:16

3. The man was cursed.

To Adam he said, "Because you listened to your wife and ate fruit from the tree about which I commanded you, 'You must not eat from it,' Cursed is the ground because of you; through painful toil you will eat food from it all the days of your life. It will produce thorns and thistles for you, and you will eat the plants of the field. By the sweat of your brow you will eat your food until you return to the ground, since from it you were taken; for dust you are and to dust you will return."

—Genesis 3:17-19

4. Death was decreed.

"...but you must not eat from the tree of the knowledge of good and evil, for when you eat from it you will certainly die."

—Genesis 2:17

Ominous, is it not? Now Adam and Eve had bodies that would die. But how is it that their descendants also became the sort of beings who die?

Hmmm...this tendency to die...might it be passed down through corrupted DNA from the first man and woman?

So, the big question remains, how could mankind get out of the trouble they found themselves in?

CHAPTER 2

WRONG CHOICES

[A note as we begin: it is important to always measure what you read or hear about the Bible using only the Bible itself as your measuring stick. Always read the Bible for yourself, in order to verify, from GOD, the truth of any article written about the Bible. You can access many Bible versions at www.BibleGateway.com or at Bible Hub.]

In the Holy Bible, we read,

> *"So God created mankind in his own image, in the image of God he created them; male and female he created them."*
>
> —Genesis 1:27

Why would GOD make a creature in His own image? Might it be that GOD wanted a creature He could relate to? To communicate with, to care about, to do things for, and most of all, to love?

But things did not go smoothly, and this is because GOD also gave the creature the ability to make choices. As we know, choices can be made well, or they can be made poorly. And poorly made choices can have very bad results.

We saw proof of this shortly after GOD created Adam and Eve, the first man and woman, when they were faced with making their first important choice.

Some wrong choices have small consequences, but unfortunately the choice made by Adam and Eve brought long-term consequences—not only for them, but for all their descendants: for you and for me and for all the people on Earth!

CHAPTER 3

THE PURPOSE
OF THE GOSPEL

The purpose of the Gospel is to deal with our problem of death.

Everyone who has ever been born has a great fear of death. The reality that death awaits all of us was brought about by the disobedient actions of Adam and Eve. The Gospel is good news from our loving GOD: it tells us that we no longer need to die. We have a choice now. We can choose life and avoid the death sentence given to all descendants of Adam and Eve.

> *For God so loved the world that he gave his one and only Son, that whoever believes in him shall not perish but have eternal life.*
>
> —John 3:16

GOD made a way out for us!

So why is it that we need to be saved from dying? What did we do to deserve it?

It all began with Adam and Eve.

Adam and Eve broke the very first law that GOD required them to keep. A law always has a penalty or a punishment, a kind of cause and effect. So how does that affect us, the descendants of Adam and Eve? It is in the corrupted DNA that we got from them.

Remember that according to science, your parents combined their DNA in order to conceive you. They, in turn, got their DNA from their parents (your grandparents), and so it went, back and back through previous generations. Go back far enough, and you'll see that we all got our DNA from our very first ancestors, Adam and Eve! Oh... so *that* is why GOD considers us to be sinful? Because we are direct descendants of Adam and Eve? Yes! We are *born sinful*, even though we have not been in jail or committed crimes. Our DNA proves it!

Now, GOD knew that we are all goners—and He didn't want to leave us in that condition! There was only one way to undo the inevitable punishments of our corrupted DNA and of death: GOD would replace our bad DNA with His perfect DNA; He would perhaps remove that corrupted DNA that causes death. GOD had a plan to help us.

Why would GOD go to all the trouble of helping us out of our DNA problem? Because He did not create mankind just on a whim. No, His purpose in making us was so we could be the recipients of His love!

On this subject, I also recommend that you read:

http://www.christianitytoday.com/edstetzer/2015/june/what-is-gospel.html, by Ed Stetzer.

https://carm.org/what-gospel, by Matt Slick.

http://www.desiringgod.org/articles/what-is-the-christian-gospel, by John Piper.

http://www.cuttingedge.org/news/salvation.html: *How do I know that I am saved? a self-test.*

CHAPTER 4

WHAT NOW?

What should you do, now that you are a Christian?

Let me try to answer that with a story. I was watching a program on TV where a Christian singer shared her testimony. She said that when she was young, she was good enough at singing that she was encouraged make it her profession.

Thinking hard about it, she decided not to become a gospel singer, because she felt she would never get anywhere doing that. So instead, she went to New York to follow her dream. Over the next several years she had many, many wonderful opportunities. But without fail, every single opportunity fell through.

Finally, one day, a chauffeur who happened to be driving her around shared that he'd had a dream about her the night before. He had dreamed about her past life, and all the disappointments she'd had. And about how, despite all her great career breaks, all her opportunities always failed to materialize into success. He indicated that she needed to rethink her approach to her life if she wanted to experience satisfaction.

The thought entered her mind then that the road to success was not in going to New York. Instead, as a Christian, the only way for her to really achieve success was to live for Jesus. When she became a Christian, she hadn't been aware that her conversion had transformed her in such a way that she would only find satisfaction in doing what she was created to do. But now she saw that any other way would never give her the peace and contentment she craved—never mind success!

She began to turn her thoughts away from the world and to focus on Christ. Bit by bit, she began to feel more satisfaction as she used gospel songs to worship GOD. She realized that true Christian living must put Christ first, and that this would give her the feeling of fulfilment that she had been seeking her entire life.

Today, Naomi Schreimer is a successful gospel singer. When you see her perform, you can see her shining, happy face, filled with satisfaction at her place in life.

CHAPTER 5

God's Plan to Help

GOD formulated a plan to help us out of our predicament of death. He did this because of His infinite love for us. He knew we are unable to help ourselves. GOD, in His infinite mercy and grace, found us a way out.

The definition of *mercy*, as it's used in the Bible, is: "More kindness than is deserved. Something for which to be thankful" (definition from *World Book Discover*).

The definition of *grace* as it's used in the Bible is: "The power of God to do for us what we cannot do for ourselves" (definition from Bible Timelines).

And the fact is, we cannot do anything for ourselves. Jesus says, "Apart from me you can do nothing" (John 15:5b).

GOD loves us so much that He wants to shower us with His love! But because we are essentially corrupted and thus sinful, we cannot be in the presence of a Holy GOD. However, GOD formulated a way to make us holy, in order for us to be with Him as He intended.

For God so loved the world that he gave his one and only Son, that whoever believes in him shall not perish but have eternal life.

—John 3:16

It was not easy for GOD to do this. In order to accomplish His plan, He had to sacrifice His only Son.

And so Jesus also suffered outside the city gate to make the people holy through his own blood.

—Hebrews 13:12

But we do see Jesus, who was made lower than the angels for a little while, now crowned with glory and honor because he suffered death, so that by the grace of God he might taste death for everyone.

—Hebrews 2:9

In bringing many sons and daughters to glory, it was fitting that God, for whom and through whom everything exists, should make the pioneer of their salvation perfect through what he suffered.

—Hebrews 2:10

Jesus, the one and only Son of GOD, suffered for us.

Then the governor's soldiers took Jesus into the Praetorium and gathered the whole company of soldiers around him. They stripped him and put a scarlet robe on him, and then twisted together a crown of thorns and set it on his head. They put a staff in his right hand. Then they knelt in front of him and mocked him. "Hail, king of the Jews!" they said.

They spit on him, and took the staff and struck him on his head again and again. After they had mocked him, they took off the robe and put his own clothes on him. Then they led him away to crucify him.
—Matthew 27:27-31

...the chief priests, the teachers of the law and the elders mocked him.
—Matthew 27:41b

In the same way the rebels who were crucified with him also heaped insults on him.
—Matthew 27:44

About three in the afternoon Jesus cried out in a loud voice, "Eli, Eli, lema sabachthani?" (which means "My God, my God, why have you forsaken me?").
—Matthew 27:46

Can you imagine how truly agonizing it must have been for Jesus, the Holy Son of God, to be separated from His Holy Father, even for one moment, and to take on the burden of the filth of the sins of the whole world? He did that for you, for me, and for every single person born into this world—all of us who are or were trapped in a corrupted body and soul and mind.

CHAPTER 6

SALVATION FOLLOWED BY BAPTISM

You have prayed to GOD, accepted that Jesus died in your place and in payment for your sins, and you choose now to turn your back on sin, giving your life over to GOD. You are saved. You have salvation.

So what comes next? You need to follow your salvation with baptism.

> *And so John the Baptist appeared in the wilderness, preaching a baptism of repentance for the forgiveness of sins.*
>
> —Mark 1:4

And your baptism can be a full water-immersion baptism, following Jesus in the manner in which He was baptized. After all, followers should do what the person they are following does, right? Sure, some people believe that sprinkling of water or pouring water onto the head is a baptism, but unfortunately that is not the way it was done in the Bible. Those methods are inventions of mankind, and are not scriptural. If baptism represents a regeneration of life, the sprinkling or pouring of water does not give that image, whereas full water immersion does.

Why full immersion, you ask? When you are completely immersed in the water, the water covers your head so you cannot breathe, and thus you "drown." That action symbolizes your death. When you are lifted up out of the water and you can breathe again, you have been "resurrected" from death into life in Christ.

> We were therefore buried with him through baptism into death in order that, just as Christ was raised from the dead through the glory of the Father, we too may live a new life.
>
> —Romans 6:4

Your "death" under the water ended your first life, during which you had lived without GOD. Your rise out of the water means that you have been born again—that from this time onward, you have a new life, living to follow Jesus Christ.

> ...and this water symbolizes baptism that now saves you also—not the removal of dirt from the body but the pledge of a clear conscience toward God. It saves you by the resurrection of Jesus Christ...
>
> —1 Peter 3:21

To follow Christ is to imitate Him and copy what He says and does. Also, we are to learn how to obey Him, as GOD has laid down in the Bible. Jesus showed us that He recommends baptism, because He actually did it Himself!

"I baptize you with water for repentance. But after me comes one who is more powerful than I, whose sandals I am not worthy to carry. He will baptize you with the Holy Spirit and fire."

—Matthew 3:11

As soon as Jesus was baptized, he went up out of the water. At that moment heaven was opened, and he saw the Spirit of God descending like a dove and alighting on him.

—Matthew 3:16

Jesus said to them, "You will drink the cup I drink and be baptized with the baptism I am baptized with."

—Mark 10:39b

Peter replied, "Repent and be baptized, every one of you, in the name of Jesus Christ for the forgiveness of your sins. And you will receive the gift of the Holy Spirit."

—Acts 2:38

As it was with Jesus, at baptism we are filled with the Holy Spirit. It is the Holy Spirit in us who will work through us to do GOD's will on Earth. But also as it was with Jesus...

Then Jesus was led by the Spirit into the wilderness to be tempted by the devil.

—Matthew 4:1

...we too, will be tempted by the devil and the lure of the world after we are baptized. That will be our period of testing, to strengthen us spiritually. This testing can show whether or not you truly believe in what Jesus did on the cross on your behalf, and its importance to you.

It was after His baptism that Jesus started His ministry of preaching. For you too, the time after your baptism can be the start of your ministry of serving GOD.

> *From that time on Jesus began to preach, "Repent, for the kingdom of heaven has come near."*
> —Matthew 4:17

Jesus started His ministry after being baptized, and you also will follow your baptism by sharing the good news of Jesus and His coming to pay for our sins, which He did by dying on the cross.

> *Then Jesus came to them and said, "All authority in heaven and on earth has been given to me. Therefore go and make disciples of all nations, baptizing them in the name of the Father and of the Son and of the Holy Spirit, and teaching them to obey everything I have commanded you. And surely I am with you always, to the very end of the age."*
> —Matthew 28:18-20

We are given the Holy Spirit, who lives inside us, to teach and guide us in our lives as Christians.

> *The Spirit searches all things, even the deep things of God. For who knows a person's thoughts except their own spirit within them? In the same way no one knows the thoughts of God except the Spirit of God. What we have received is not the spirit of the*

world, but the Spirit who is from God, so that we may understand what God has freely given us. This is what we speak, not in words taught us by human wisdom but in words taught by the Spirit, explaining spiritual realities with Spirit-taught words. The person without the Spirit does not accept the things that come from the Spirit of God but considers them foolishness, and cannot understand them because they are discerned only through the Spirit. The person with the Spirit makes judgments about all things, but such a person is not subject to merely human judgments, for, "Who has known the mind of the Lord so as to instruct him?" But we have the mind of Christ.

—1 Corinthians 2:10b-16

Be careful that you do not resist the Holy Spirit, but allow Him to work through you. You will know that the Holy Spirit is motivating you when your thoughts and actions line up with what is taught in the Bible, GOD's Word.

CHAPTER 7

SUMMARY OF THE GOSPEL

1. You are separated permanently from GOD and suffer death because of broken law.

   As it is written: "There is no one righteous, not even one; there is no one who understands; there is no one who seeks God."

   —Romans 3:10-11

   They will be punished with everlasting destruction and shut out from the presence of the Lord and from the glory of his might.

   —2 Thessalonians 1:9

   All of us also lived among them at one time, gratifying the cravings of our flesh and following its desires and thoughts. Like the rest, we were by nature deserving of wrath.

   —Ephesians 2:3

But your iniquities have separated you from your God; your sins have hidden his face from you, so that he will not hear.

—Isaiah 59:2

2. Jesus is the only One who can be our Saviour, paying for our death penalty that was incurred when the law was broken.

…for all have sinned and fall short of the glory of God, and all are justified freely by his grace through the redemption that came by Christ Jesus.

—Romans 3:23-24

For the wages of sin is death, but the gift of God is eternal life in Christ Jesus our Lord.

—Romans 6:23

Salvation is found in no one else, for there is no other name under heaven given to mankind by which we must be saved.

—Acts 4:12

Jesus answered, "I am the way and the truth and the life. No one comes to the Father except through me."

—John 14:6

The Word became flesh and made his dwelling among us. We have seen his glory, the glory of the one and only Son, who came from the Father, full of grace and truth.

—John 1:14

3. Jesus bore our sins on Himself to satisfy the punishment for the broken law and to restore us to GOD.

   "He himself bore our sins" in his body on the cross, so that we might die to sins and live for righteousness; "by his wounds you have been healed."
   —1 Peter 2:24

   For what I received I passed on to you as of first importance: that Christ died for our sins according to the Scriptures, that he was buried, that he was raised on the third day according to the Scriptures...
   —1 Corinthians 15:3-4

4. **Your time has come! GOD is calling you!**

   He went on to say, "This is why I told you that no one can come to me unless the Father has enabled them."
   —John 6:65

   "The time has come," he said. "The kingdom of God has come near. Repent and believe the good news!"
   —Mark 1:15

Read this explanation of the Gospel (excerpted from this article, https://carm.org/what-gospel, by Matt Slick) to understand more:

"It is only through Jesus that we can escape the penalty that God will execute upon all who have broken His holy and perfect law. Do you want to be saved from the righteous judgment of God? If so, if you want to become a Christian and follow God, then you must realize that you have sinned against God and are

under His judgment. You must look to Jesus who died on the cross and trust what He did in order for you to be forgiven of your sentence and be saved from the judgment of God. This is accomplished by faith alone in what Jesus has done. You cannot add any human works to what Jesus has done.

"If you desire to receive Christ, we offer the following prayer as an example. It is not a formula, but it is a representation of what it means to trust in Christ."

[If you want to accept Christ as your Lord and Saviour, say this prayer aloud.]

"'Lord Jesus. I come to you and confess that I am a sinner, that I have lied, thought evil in my heart, and broken your law. Please forgive me of my sins.'

"'I trust in what you have done on the cross, and I receive you. I believe that you have died on the cross, was buried, and rose from the dead for my sins. Please cleanse me of my sin and be the Lord of my life. I trust you completely for the forgiveness of my sins and put no trust in my own efforts of righteousness. Lord Jesus, please save me as I receive you and believe what you did on the cross is the only way to be saved from the righteous judgment of God the Father. Amen.' If you have prayed the prayer truthfully and faithfully, then you have obeyed Christ and believed the gospel (Mark 1:15). You've done so because God has granted that you come to Christ (John 6:65), *worked belief in you (John 6:29), and granted that you believe (Phil. 1:29).*

"Now tell others about your commitment to Jesus. The Bible says, "if you confess with your mouth Jesus as Lord, and believe in your heart that God raised Him from the dead, you shall be saved; for with the heart man believes, resulting in righteousness, and with the mouth he confesses, resulting in salvation" (ROM. 10:9-10)."

I also recommend that you read:

- What is the Gospel (Christianity Today article) by Ed Stetzer.
- What is the Gospel (Christian Apologetics and Research Ministry). by Matt Slick.
- What is the Christian Gospel (Desiring God ministries) by John Piper.

Now that you have your salvation, your commitment to Jesus Christ can be publicly shown through your act of baptism.

CHAPTER **8**

PUTTING CHRIST FIRST

Well, where do we go to find out how to put Christ first? GOD's Word, the Holy Bible, of course! There are many things that a Christian, who follows GOD, needs to know and have. These things make up what is called being "in Christ."

First of all, if you love GOD, you should know we have an enemy who doesn't like that! This is the fallen angel, Satan. He is called *Lucifer* in the Bible, and also called *Beelzebub*, *Belial*, Deceiver, etc., and his main purpose is to make us Christians miserable and ultimately to destroy us! And, in addition, we also have our old physical bodies to contend with. After all, our minds have some help from the Holy Spirit, but our bodies are still at the mercy of our sinful desires and the world around us.

So, you might say, we need help for our insides and for our outsides!

Well, that is where the armor of GOD comes in. "Hmmm," you might say. "Armor...isn't that something that covers our heads, bodies, and feet, like in the Middle Ages? Knights and castles and all that?" Yes, and you will find that GOD uses that exact illustration in the Bible to show us how to protect our bodies from spiritual harm. "But they used to use the armor in battles with swords, axes, and swinging iron balls with spikes! Yikes! What are we going to be fighting? Battles?" Well, yes, and you can call that Spiritual Warfare 101.

"Whoa!" you say. "I am going to need a really *fantastic* suit of armor, if I am going to be fighting like some knight of the round table!" Well, GOD has provided exactly *that* for us in His Word, and you can read about it in the book of Ephesians, chapter 6, in a section about the armor of GOD:

Finally, be strong in the Lord and in his mighty power. Put on the full armor of God, so that you can take your stand against the devil's schemes. For our struggle is not against flesh and blood, but against the rulers, against the authorities, against the powers of this dark world and against the spiritual forces of evil in the heavenly realms. Therefore put on the full armor of God, so that when the day of evil comes, you may be able to stand your ground, and after you have done everything, to stand. Stand firm then, with the belt of truth buckled around your waist, with the breastplate of righteousness in place, and with your feet fitted with the readiness that comes from the gospel of peace. In addition to all this, take up the shield of faith, with which you can extinguish all the flaming arrows of the evil one. Take the helmet of salvation and the sword of the Spirit, which is the word of God.

—Ephesians 6:10-17

Protection against physical and spiritual harm is what you have when you've put on the armor of GOD.

Belt of Truth, Breastplate of Righteousness, Gospel of Peace, Shield of Faith, Helmet of Salvation, Sword of the Spirit. Good set of armor, wouldn't you say? But of course, in order for it to *protect* you, you need to actually put the armor *on*! Let's talk about how you do that, piece by piece.

Truth - Everything that GOD says in His Word, the Bible, is true, every single bit. It blocks out falsehood. So we read the Bible from cover to cover to find out what *is* true.

Righteousness - If our heart is covered with GOD's holiness, nothing can get past it to end us. So we accept Christ as our Saviour so He can indwell us (or come into our bodies), so we can live forever.

Gospel of Peace - Our feet will take us everywhere to spread the news that brings peace to the world. That can only come through GOD. So we will be going everywhere to tell others about Jesus, who can and will bring lasting peace and happiness to the world.

Faith - With Jesus in us, we are completely protected from anything and everything that Satan does to us. So we believe all that GOD tells us in His Word, and do not have any doubts that can put holes in our defenses, allowing the enemy to come into our life. We trust GOD!

Salvation - Jesus dying on the Cross saved us from the real deadly results of bad DNA and gave us GOD's perfect DNA, which negates or removes the bad DNA.

(So the punishment that caused all of us to suffer death, was suffered by Jesus instead, but *only* if we choose to accept Jesus' DNA fix. In fact, Jesus died in our place so we could take the "fix"—but each of us has to do it for ourselves. Other people cannot do it for us—not parents, siblings, relatives, or any other well-intentioned person!)

Sword of the Spirit - This is Jesus, who has defeated our enemy Satan, and has also eliminated Death for us. So we already have the victory over Death and Satan, but we must be in Christ for this victory to be true.

> *Circumcise your hearts, therefore, and do not be stiff-necked any longer.*
> —Deuteronomy 10:16

> *The LORD your God will circumcise your hearts and the hearts of your descendants, so that you may love him with all your heart and with all your soul, and live.*
> —Deuteronomy 30:6

> *The law of their God is in their hearts; their feet do not slip.*
> —Psalm 37:31

> *Those who live according to the flesh have their minds set on what the flesh desires; but those who live in accordance with the Spirit have their minds set on what the Spirit desires. The mind governed by the flesh is death, but the mind governed by the Spirit is life and peace.*
> —Romans 8:5-6

He answered, "Love the Lord your God with all your heart and with all your soul and with all your strength and with all your mind; and, 'Love your neighbor as yourself.'"

—Luke 10:27

To fill our hearts, minds, souls, and bodies with the Word of GOD, we read the Bible.

There are many books in the New Testament section of the Bible, and those teach us how to live our life as Christians, how to be "in" Christ. A favorite of many Christians is the book of Romans. The first half of Romans tells you all about who and what GOD is, about the family of GOD, about the Father, the Son, and the Holy Spirit. The second half teaches you how to conduct yourself as a Christian, how to keep GOD close to you. All the books following Romans, up to just before Revelation, are worth the read for those reasons.

When you dive into the ocean for a swim, the water literally surrounds every inch of your body—not to mention your ears, nose, and mouth! In the same way, we must immerse ourselves in GOD's Word. People around you will notice a change as you strive to be in Christ.

Let Christ surround you and permeate you by reading GOD's Word, praying for GOD to reveal what the words mean, and applying the Word to your life right away.

Drink from the well of living water.

What does it mean to be in Christ?

Create in me a pure heart, O God, and renew a steadfast spirit within me.

—Psalm 51:10

...but those who hope in the LORD will renew their strength. They will soar on wings like eagles; they will run and not grow weary, they will walk and not be faint.

—Isaiah 40:31

Do not conform to the pattern of this world, but be transformed by the renewing of your mind. Then you will be able to test and approve what God's will is— his good, pleasing and perfect will.

—Romans 12:2

For you have been born again, not of perishable seed, but of imperishable, through the living and enduring word of God.

—1 Peter 1:23

Therefore, if anyone is in Christ, the new creation has come: The old has gone, the new is here!

—2 Corinthians 5:17

What can we look forward to?

...I will give you hidden treasures, riches stored in secret places, so that you will know I am the LORD, the God of Israel, who summons you by name.

—Isaiah 45:3

Being in Christ changes your DNA!

CHAPTER 9

SHARING THE GOSPEL

Once you become a Christian, you will need to obey Christ in what is called the Great Commission. Here is Christ's instruction to us:

> *Then Jesus came to them and said, "All authority in heaven and on earth has been given to me. Therefore go and make disciples of all nations, baptizing them in the name of the Father and of the Son and of the Holy Spirit, and teaching them to obey everything I have commanded you. And surely I am with you always, to the very end of the age.*
> —Matthew 28:18-20

To start sharing, pray first to ask the Holy Spirit to teach you how to share. And you need to pray also for the person you want to share with. That enables the Holy Spirit to go ahead of you to prepare the heart of that person to accept the news of GOD's gift of salvation. Pray that the Holy Spirit gives you the words to say.

We are born resisting GOD. Do you notice how a baby's first spoken word is not always "Mama" but is often "No!"? Since we are separated from GOD, we must have our hard hearts softened by the Holy Spirit before we can accept anything that is of GOD. When you attempt to share the Gospel without the preparation of the Holy Spirit, you will always meet resistance and hostility!

After prayer, you need to ensure the right timing in approaching that person. Don't do it just after a funeral, and not when the person is preoccupied or otherwise upset and in a distracted state of mind. Perhaps you might find a setting where the person is more receptive. Invite your friend—and this should be someone with whom you've already established a good relationship—to dinner, or some other quiet event, away from distractions.

Share with that person how your life has changed, tell them what a really good thing has happened to you! Tell about a Bible verse that really touched your heart—maybe John 3:16: *"For God so loved the world that he gave his one and only Son, that whoever believes in him shall not perish but have eternal life."*

Tell your friend that you found there is a real GOD, whose love for us is so great that He would send his only Son to die for us. No fake god could ever do that! Is there even a human parent who would do that? Christ's sacrifice shows the extreme love this GOD feels for us. You could go on to say, "And the best thing about it is that we will be able to live forever! Wouldn't you like to cheat death and live forever? How can that happen? All you need to do is to bow your head and pray with me, *'Yes, GOD, I believe that your son, Jesus, paid for my death when he died on the cross in my place. I do not want to be separated from You anymore, GOD! I want you to be my GOD; I want to love and obey You. Amen.'"*

Say to your friend, "You will be entered by the Holy Spirit. Before you became a Christian, you were resistant to GOD. Now you have been born again. That means the Holy Spirit comes inside you, and joins with your human spirit to make your heart receptive to GOD's teachings from the Bible, His Word. Before, to you, reading the Bible was like reading a bunch of nice stories. Now, you will actually learn from GOD's Holy Spirit! So be sure to read the Bible daily! Life will never be the same!"

CHAPTER **10**

YOUR NEW LIFE

I was watching a sermon on TV one Sunday and was moved by the message that many people feel empty and lonely. Some have every material thing they could possibly want and yet are still empty and lonely. Some have tried to get everything and are repeatedly unsuccessful. We can see this same lesson in the Bible story about the woman at the well:

> *When a Samaritan woman came to draw water, Jesus said to her, "Will you give me a drink?" (His disciples had gone into the town to buy food.)*

> *The Samaritan woman said to him, "You are a Jew and I am a Samaritan woman. How can you ask me for a drink?" (Jews did not associate with Samaritans.)*

> *Jesus answered her, "If you knew the gift of God and who it is that asks you for a drink, you would have asked him and he would have given you living water."*

"Sir" the woman said, "you have nothing to draw with and the well is deep. Where can you get this living water? Are you greater than our father Jacob, who gave us the well and drank from it himself, as did also his sons and his livestock?"

—John 4:7-12

This woman had spent her life drawing water from a well that never produced the results that she wanted. Like most people, she looked for love, respect, and acceptance. Having had five husbands, she continuously found rejection and disappointment. She was alone at the well because none of the other townswomen accepted her.

Now Jesus came along and offered her something that she really needed—He offered to give her what she had wanted her whole life. He offered her living water that would satisfy her completely and lead her to a fulfilling life.

The lesson in this story is that we, Christians, often fall into the old habit of drinking from the old well. We fall into our old habits of following the materialistic ways of the world around us, totally ignoring God. Then we get disappointed with the results we see in our lives. But what can we expect, if we still are drinking from the old wells? The world's wells will never bring true spiritual happiness and satisfaction because they only feed our physical needs, when we also need fulfillment of our spiritual needs.

We are all both physical and spiritual. The world seeks to satisfy the physical, choosing to ignore the spiritual, or discrediting the spiritual as nonexistent. Jesus came to fill the empty spiritual void in us, to make us whole, as God had created us to be.

On the one hand, the woman drank from a well (an analogy for her disappointing life) that did nothing to satisfy. On the other hand, Jesus offered drink from a well that had everything she was made to want and desire. There is the old well, which only offers unsatisfying things, and there is the new well, which can offer everything that satisfies and more.

Resist drinking from the old well! Drink from the new well to get that feeling of deep satisfaction and fulfillment that we all long for deep down. This means putting our spiritual life first. Then other people will be attracted to us, because they will sense in us what they are missing in themselves.

If you have been a Christian for a while, but you somehow aren't really sure, read and follow the Bible to get more insights from the Holy Spirit. What you are missing could very well be the Spirit!

SECTION 2

THE AWESOMENESS OF GOD

CHAPTER 11

THE TRI-UNITY OF GOD

Where do we get the idea that GOD is one GOD in three Persons? The Bible talks about the *oneness* of GOD, so we know it is true that GOD is one.

Deuteronomy 6:4b says, *"The LORD our God, the LORD is one."*

Galatians 3:20b says, *"God is one."*

1 Timothy 2:5a says, *"For there is one God."*

James 2:19 says, *"You believe that there is one God. Good! Even the demons believe that-and shudder."*

But at the same time, the Bible also talks about the *three distinct persons* of the Father, the Son, and the Holy Spirit, telling us about the special ways that each of Them relates to mankind.

2 Corinthians 13:14 says, *"May the grace of the Lord Jesus Christ, and the love of God, and the fellowship of the Holy Spirit be with you all."*

1 Peter 1:2b says, "*...chosen according to the foreknowledge of God the Father, through the sanctifying work of the Spirit, for obedience to Jesus Christ.*"

The Bible also ties the Father and the Son and the Holy Spirit together as inseparable Entities, showing that all at the same time are the oneness of GOD.

Matthew 28:19b says, "*...baptizing them in the name of the Father and of the Son and of the Holy Spirit.*" (Note that the word "name" is singular, meaning one name applies to all three.)

Revelation 21:22b says, "*...for the Lord God Almighty and the Lamb are the temple of it...*" (Note that "temple" is singular, but that "temple" refers to both.)

Revelation 22:1b says, "*...proceeding out of the throne of God and of the Lamb.*" (Note that "throne" is singular, and the "throne" is occupied by both.)

In Genesis we read, "*Then God said, 'Let us make mankind in our image, in our likeness'*" (Gen. 1:26a). ("Us" here refers to the Trinity.)

Finally, Genesis 1:27 reads, "*So God created mankind in his own image.*" (Here, "his" refers to the oneness of GOD.)

GOD would not give a truth in two seemingly opposite ways unless both ways really described the same truth. This is a "mystery" of GOD that we humans find hard to understand!

CHAPTER 12

GOD Is YAHWEH

YAHWEH. Israel's sacred word for GOD is Y*HW*H. In this word, Hebrew vowel letters are not used and are unknown. But there are some things we do know. We know that YAHWEH is:

1. The One.

   Deuteronomy 6:4 says, *"Hear, O Israel: The Lord our God, the Lord is one."*

   (This means GOD is number One in all the universe.)

2. The Ultimate.

   Psalm 97:9 says, *"For you, Lord, are the Most High over all the earth; you are exalted far above all gods."*

   Isaiah 40:12 says, *"Who has measured the waters in the hollow of his hand, or with the breadth of his hand marked off the heavens? Who has held the dust of the earth in a basket, or weighed the mountains on the scales and the hills in a balance?"*

(GOD is the very first of the very best!)

3. An Eternal Being.

   Psalm 90:2 says, "Before the mountains were born or you brought forth the whole world, from everlasting to everlasting you are God."

   (GOD has always been around!)

4. The Creator.

   Genesis 1:1–2 says, *"In the beginning God created the heavens and the earth. Now the earth was formless and empty, darkness was over the surface of the deep, and the Spirit of God was hovering over the waters."*

   John 1:3 says, *"Through him all things were made; without him nothing was made that has been made."*

   (GOD made every single thing!)

5. The Ruler.

   Psalm 115:3 says, *"Our God is in heaven; he does whatever pleases him."*

   (GOD is in charge of everything!)

6. The Sustainer of all that exists.

Job 38:4 says, *"Where were you when I laid the earth's foundation? Tell me, if you understand."*

(Read the entire chapter 38 of Job, and you will see that GOD keeps everything in creation working properly!)

There are many idols and there are people that say those idols should be worshipped. But there is only *one* real Creator who is *able* to save you from death. He is the one that made us into living, breathing people. He is the one that keeps you alive and living! And He is really interested in you, His creation!

Because of who He is, not only must you be very thankful to Him, your Creator, but you need to show Him your trust by relying on Him for help in your daily life. Rely on Him with your family and friendships, and for absolutely everything that you need. GOD wants you to let Him do *everything*! In fact, there is nothing that He will ignore. He will never ever say, *"Go away...I'm busy, come back later!"* or *"Do not come to Me with something so unimportant!"*

GOD will always say with love, "I'm 'all ears'—what do you need, My child? I will always do My best for you!"

CHAPTER 13

GOD Is Not a Religion

There are many deeply religious people in the world, full of wisdom, love, peace, etc. What does GOD think of them? His Word tells us.

> Romans 3:23 says, *"For all have sinned and fall short of the glory of God."*

> Galatians 3:22 says, *"But the Scripture declares that the whole world is a prisoner of sin, so that what was promised, being given through faith in Jesus Christ, might be given to those who believe."*

Clearly GOD's Word teaches that even the most highly revered men in our world are not able to meet His standards for holiness. But you might say, "All these men have many of those good spiritual qualities described in the Bible, so why aren't they up to GOD's standards? Do they not behave with and emulate all Christlike qualities?"

Let's compare GOD's standard for holiness with mankind's standard for holiness. Man sees a person espousing love, peace, and harmony, living it and telling others to do the same, and calls that person holy. But GOD says that man can only become holy by following His formula for holiness. GOD needs man to recognize his total helplessness and inability to become holy on his own, and to place his complete trust in GOD, accepting Christ as Saviour, and being spiritually reborn into GOD's own holy family.

> *Clearly no one is justified before God by the law, because, "The righteous will live by faith."*
> —Galatians 3:11

This verse says it all. Whenever man has tried on his own to be holy by following the law, he has never succeeded for long. It was always temporary, and all his efforts only have an effect in his immediate physical world. A look at world history confirms this. Man, being a physical being, shortsightedly does many "works" that temporarily influence this physical world, not realizing that "life" was not meant to be solely the short life lived in just our physical bodies.

Not admitting that there is a GOD, man arrogantly goes forth on his own to fix all the wrongs in this world, albeit unsuccessfully. If man did succeed in "fixing" everything, that would only account for a fraction of the lifespan that GOD had meant for him. But what about the millions of years he was meant to live? Focusing on his physical existence and ignoring his eternal one has been the second biggest mistake of mankind since the Fall in the Garden of Eden.

Religion without GOD has no validity, no substance, and no power for permanent change. Religion without

GOD is a manmade religion formed from man's own concepts of who GOD might be, and what he would *like* GOD to be. Religion is an empty shell of holiness, easily broken. Religion without GOD is designed to make man look "good," to prove that man only needs himself—that he is "GOD."

Isn't that why man spends his whole life inventing, making, creating, discovering? By behaving in a "god-like" manner, man hopes to make his own way to godhood.

What exactly is "religion without GOD"? It is having all the trappings of godliness without giving credit to the one true GOD. How do we give credit to the one true GOD? We follow His instructions for becoming holy. We adhere to His methodology only. We accept Jesus as our Saviour so that we can be reborn spiritually into GOD's holy family. We let GOD make us holy. We accept that we cannot ever do it on our own.

So we must not be distracted from GOD by so-called "holy" men. To focus only on the trappings of holiness can be fatal. To focus on the true source of holiness can be eternally beneficial!

After all, man is really both physical and spiritual. Let us not emphasize the former and neglect the latter. The former is just for a few short years, the latter is for all eternity!

Focus on Jesus, and accept Him as your Saviour. Then follow His ways, emulate Him, and watch how GOD will change the world through you!

CHAPTER 14

WHAT IS OUR GOD LIKE?

GOD is the one and only GOD that exists anywhere.

Isaiah 44:6 says, *"This is what the LORD says—Israel's King and Redeemer, the LORD Almighty: I am the first and I am the last; apart from me there is no God."*

1. He never changes, and cannot be changed.

    James 1:17 says, *"Every good and perfect gift is from above, coming down from the Father of the heavenly lights, who does not change like shifting shadows."*

2. He is invisible.

    Colossians 1:15 says, *"The Son is the image of the invisible God, the firstborn over all creation."*

3. He had no beginning and has no end.

    1 Kings 8:27 says, *"But will God really dwell on earth? The heavens, even the highest heaven, cannot contain you. How much less this temple I have built!"*

4. He is absolutely perfect.

   Matthew 5:48 says, *"Be perfect, therefore, as your heavenly Father is perfect."*

5. He is Spirit.

   John 4:24 says, *"God is spirit, and his worshipers must worship in the Spirit and in truth."*

6. He is totally holy.

   1 Peter 1:15-16 says, *"But just as he who called you is holy, so be holy in all you do; for it is written: 'Be holy, because I am holy.'"*

7. He is motivated one hundred percent by love.

   1 John 4:8–12 says, *"Whoever does not love does not know God, because God is love. This is how God showed his love among us: He sent his one and only Son into the world that we might live through him. This is love: not that we loved God, but that he loved us and sent his Son as an atoning sacrifice for our sins. Dear friends, since God so loved us, we also ought to love one another. No one has ever seen God; but if we love one another, God lives in us and his love is made complete in us."*

8. He is one hundred percent truthful in all He does.

   John 3:33 says, *"Whoever has accepted it has certified that God is truthful."*

9. He is one GOD in three distinct Persons.

   Matthew 28:19 says, *"Therefore go and make disciples of all nations, baptizing them in the name of the Father and of the Son and of the Holy Spirit."*

   (Note that the name is singular, yet it applies to all three Persons.)

10. He came down to earth in a physical form.

   John 1:14 says, *"The Word became flesh and made his dwelling among us. We have seen his glory, the glory of the one and only Son, who came from the Father, full of grace and truth."*

Look up the words *holy*, *eternal*, and *spirit* in the dictionary. If you take a closer look at *many* of the descriptions of GOD, you can see that He is the only Being that can be described in all those ways. GOD is very unique, One of a kind!

The above is just a very tiny, tiny, short list of attributes that describe our GOD. The real list is much, much longer and totally endless! Even if we decided to not believe in GOD, He would *still* be there! He does not *need* us to believe or acknowledge that He exists. He exists anyways! There is *so much* to know about GOD, that we can never ever find out EVERYTHING there is to know about Him!

SECTION 3

THE HOLY SPIRIT

CHAPTER 15

WHO IS THE HOLY SPIRIT?

The Holy Spirit is one of the three persons who together are the one GOD. The other two persons are the Father and the Son. They each have special jobs to do as GOD. God, the Father, who oversees everything; God, the Son, who does the work of salvation; God, the Holy Spirit, who lives in us to help us become more like Christ in spirit and in body.

> *Therefore go and make disciples of all nations, baptizing them in the name of the Father and of the Son and of the Holy Spirit.*
> —Matthew 28:19

> *Then Peter said, "Ananias, how is it that Satan has so filled your heart that you have lied to the Holy Spirit and have kept for yourself some of the money you received for the land? Didn't it belong to you before it was sold? And after it was sold, wasn't the money at your disposal? What made you think of doing such a thing? You have not lied just to human beings but to God."*
> —Acts 5:3-4 (emphasis mine)

Examine yourselves to see whether you are in the faith; test yourselves. Do you not realize that Christ Jesus is in you—unless, of course, you fail the test? And I trust that you will discover that we have not failed the test. Now we pray to God that you will not do anything wrong—not so that people will see that we have stood the test but so that you will do what is right even though we may seem to have failed. For we cannot do anything against the truth, but only for the truth.

—2 Corinthians 13:5-8

Since the Holy Spirit is a spirit, He cannot be seen by us using our eyes, or touched by us using our hands. Yet the Holy Spirit is able to be with us at all times after we have accepted Jesus as our Saviour. The Holy Spirit merges with our own human spirit at the time when we pray individually to accept GOD's gift of salvation.

In order to have the Holy Spirit in us, we need to have accepted Jesus. The Holy Spirit will then be within us, and His ministry is to help and to teach us. Because He is holy, we must meet Him on "holy ground." That is to say, He cannot be where sin is. Accepting Jesus removes our sins and makes us sinless and holy, so that the Holy Spirit is able to come to teach and to help us.

People who do not accept Jesus do not have the Holy Spirit. They are separated from the Holy Spirit's presence because of their sin. Jesus paid for our sins, so we do not have anything separating us from GOD's Holy Spirit.

"Well," you say, "what about those sins I keep doing even *after* I have accepted Christ?" My answer is: *that* is why the Holy Spirit comes into every believer. Every time you commit a sin that you know about, always pray and admit to GOD that you are sorry for that sin. And right away, the Holy Spirit will clean that sin right out of your spirit and body, so that you will remain holy and acceptable to GOD.

"Well," you might ask, "what happens if I do not say 'sorry' to GOD when I have sinned?" The answer is that sin will cause lots of problems for you. It will rot you spiritually, and may cause you to be so tied up inside that you may even become sick physically.

Remember that sin happens when we are not following GOD and His ways. But the Holy Spirit both helps us not to sin, and helps to clean us after we do fall into sin. *Whew*! What a relief! Thank You, GOD! Come, Holy Spirit, come!

CHAPTER 16

JESUS SENDS HIS HOLY SPIRIT TO US

You might ask, "Why don't I feel or behave differently after accepting Jesus?"

By now you will have noticed that, for a Christian, there are usually two sides to most things: the physical and the spiritual. Although we have accepted Christ and our glorified spiritual bodies are sure of going to live in heaven with GOD, who is Spirit, we also still have to live in our physical bodies on this earth.

Jesus knew that we needed His help to become Christlike, so when He returned to the Father in heaven, His last words to the disciples before leaving were:

> *But I tell you the truth: It is for your good that I am going away. Unless I go away, the Counselor will not come to you; but if I go, I will send him to you... When he comes, he will convict the world of guilt in regard to sin and righteousness and judgment.*
> —John 16:7-8

We are also told that the Holy Spirit would show us everything about the Trinity. GOD's power, glory, honor—*all* the things that belong to GOD—are shared by the Father, the Son, and the Holy Spirit, because GOD is one GOD, and the persons of the Trinity are separated by nothing. Remember, our DNA changes, too!

Jesus says of His Holy Spirit:

> *He will glorify me because it is from me that he will receive what he will make known to you. All that belongs to the Father is mine. That is why I said the Spirit will receive from me what he will make known to you...In a little while you will see me no more, and then after a little while you will see me.*
>
> —John 16:14-16

Jesus, the Son, was going back to the Father in heaven, but then sending His Holy Spirit. If you turn to your Bible and read *Isaiah 9:6*, you will see that one of Jesus' titles is "*Wonderful Counselor*," and another title is "*Everlasting Father*." This shows us that the Trinity is real, and that the Son, the Father, and the Holy Spirit are one God. It is like an equation that reads, *1 + 1 + 1 = 1.*

So when Jesus says, "*after a little while you will see me*," He meant just that! Jesus promises to send God, the Holy Spirit, but we always know that Jesus, the Son, is *also* there, and so is God, the Father, for that matter, for it is impossible for them to be separated!

Still puzzled? Well, think of your own *father*. He is also a *son*, when he goes to see his father. And he is a *husband* when he is with your mother. He is a *provider* for you when he goes to work for money to support your family.

Now when your dad is at work, can you say he is no longer a son or a husband or a father? When your father is just with you, is it true that he is no longer a husband or a provider? Certainly not! (Though unlike GOD, your dad is just one person!)

That is why Jesus said,

All that belongs to the Father is mine. That is why I said the Spirit will take from what is mine and make it known to you...In a little while you will see me no more, and then after a little while you will see me.
                                          —John 16:15-16

Why would Jesus send us God the Holy Spirit?

But the Counselor, the Holy Spirit, whom the Father will send in my name, will teach you all things and will remind you of everything I have said to you.
                                          —John 14:26

So the Holy Spirit is with us to teach us about GOD, and to help make us into GOD'S likeness, in the same way that a child is born to be a member of his or her own family...in every atom, molecule, thought, and action!

Keep in mind that the one and only time when Jesus was separated from God the Father and God the Holy Spirit, it was by choice, and caused by Jesus taking upon Himself the sins of the world!

CHAPTER 17

THE HOLY SPIRIT IN US

Did you know that the *Holy Spirit...*

1. *Gave BIRTH to us,* the group of Christians called the Church? When we are reborn spiritually, it is the Holy Spirit who joins with our human spirit to create our new spirit "body." This is where the "father sperm" (which is the Holy Spirit) joins with the "mother egg" (which is our human spirit) to create the "new baby" (which is us, each a new spirit in Christ).

When the day of Pentecost came, they were all together in one place. Suddenly a sound like the blowing of a violent wind came from heaven and filled the whole house where they were sitting. They saw what seemed to be tongues of fire that separated and came to rest on each of them. All of them were filled with the Holy Spirit and began to speak in other tongues as the Spirit enabled them.

—Acts 2:1-4

2. *BAPTIZES believers into the Church?* When the Holy Spirit joins the human spirit of a new believer, that new believer automatically becomes part of the Church!

   So, when you got baptized you became a part of Jesus's Church body. Just like all the cells in you make up *your* body, all the many, many believers make up what is called "the body of Christ." All the believers joined together keep the Church body going, and living, and working for GOD!

   For we were all baptized by one Spirit so as to form one body—whether Jews or Gentiles, slave or free— and we were all given the one Spirit to drink.
   —1 Corinthians 12:13

3. *LIVES WITHIN the Church?* Once the Holy Spirit has joined with our human spirit, He never ever leaves. He is permanently merged with us—living, breathing, eating, sleeping, enjoying life with us! He seals us!

   Don't you know that you yourselves are God's temple and that God's Spirit dwells in your midst?
   —1 Corinthians 3:16

   And in him you too are being built together to become a dwelling in which God lives by his Spirit.
   —Ephesians 2:22

4. *UNIFIES the Church?* That means He helps us to want to work together, to do things for each other, to agree with each other, to do everything with the same ideas and purposes in mind—that is, to give GOD glory!

Make every effort to keep the unity of the Spirit through the bond of peace. There is one body and one Spirit, just as you were called to one hope when you were called.

—Ephesians 4:3-4

5. *GIVES special SPIRIT GIFTS to the Church*? The kind of presents that the Holy Spirit gives to us have great power! If used properly, they can change people, and they can cause very good things to happen! What are some of those gifts? Teaching, leading, healing, etc. Find more of them in 1 Corinthians 12. These gifts are given to us to enable us to do GOD's work.

There are different kinds of gifts, but the same Spirit distributes them. There are different kinds of service, but the same Lord. There are different kinds of working, but in all of them and in everyone it is the same God at work.

—1 Corinthians 12:4-6

6. *PICKS people to lead the Church.* He shows people what kinds of work to do in the Church with His gifts. And, if you have the right attitude for service, it can be you!

Keep watch over yourselves and all the flock of which the Holy Spirit has made you overseers. Be shepherds of the church of God, which he bought with his own blood.

—Acts 20:28

While they were worshiping the Lord and fasting, the Holy Spirit said, "Set apart for me Barnabas and Saul for the work to which I have called them."

—Acts 13:2

7. *RESTRAINS Satan's works of evil in the world.* The Holy Spirit is within the Church body of Christ on earth to hold back or slow down the works of evil in the world until such time as Jesus returns to earth to take up (or rapture) His Bride, the Church, for the wedding and marriage feast in heaven! (See Matthew 25.)

For the secret power of lawlessness is already at work; but the one who now holds it back will continue to do so till he is taken out of the way.

—2 Thessalonians 2:7

The millions of believers in this world with the Holy Spirit living in them must make a really, really large and powerful spiritual body! Just think: since we believers are part of that vast spiritual body, the body of Christ, going against the Church would be going against GOD!

CHAPTER 18

The Holy Spirit Sanctifies Us

SANCTIFICATION: a cleaning away of our ungodly choices.

When we were little, we listened to our parents' advice and relied on their protection, and accepted all the good things they gave us. Now that we are older, we feel that we have to show that we are independent and can do things on our own!

How does that same dynamic work when it comes to our relationship with GOD?

It seems that GOD wants us to totally rely on Him, but isn't that the same as treating us like we are little kids again?

First, let us consider the pros and cons of this view.

Wouldn't it be great if we were able to make everything always turn out right? To control and decide what we get, to control the way people treat us, to control our feelings so that they are always good, to always enjoy things, to be happy? But, we can't! Still, you might say, "I really want it to be that way!"

Well, the very things that we cannot control can be made available to us by GOD. He is the one who can provide the most for us, because He wants to make us His children.

Hey, we can be adults and at the same time still rely on GOD!

All kids know that what makes adults different than kids is that adults can make their own choices. Well, GOD teaches us to make godly choices, and yet He still provides for us.

Before we accept Christ, we naturally bend towards making choices that are harmful to us. Bad choices come naturally, because choices made without GOD come naturally, as we follow after the pattern of disobedience set by Adam and Eve, our ancestors. *After* we accept Christ, the Holy Spirit changes our nature so that we *naturally* make the same kinds of choices Jesus would make.

> *Therefore, since we have these promises, dear friends, let us purify ourselves from everything that contaminates body and spirit, perfecting holiness out of reverence for God.*
> —2 Corinthians 7:1

> *But just as he who called you is holy, so be holy in all you do; for it is written: "Be holy, because I am holy."*
> —1 Peter 3:15-16

But grow in the grace and knowledge of our Lord and Savior Jesus Christ. To him be glory both now and forever! Amen.

—1 Peter 3:18

How will GOD do that? When we accept Jesus, GOD's Holy Spirit comes right into us, merging His Spirit with our spirit. He will start to change our spirits to be like His. We will begin to think and act as Jesus would. When we make our choices now, we will naturally make the kinds of choices GOD would, not because "GOD told me to do that," but because it will feel right for us to do that! *Totally painless and wonderfully amazing!*

When the Holy Spirit makes changes to our spirit, that is called *sanctification*—a kind of purifying of our spirits so that we are acceptable to GOD, and can be therefore be with Him in heaven.

And that is what some of you were. But you were washed, you were sanctified, you were justified in the name of the Lord Jesus Christ and by the Spirit of our God.

—1 Corinthians 6:11

And we also thank God continually because, when you received the word of God, which you heard from us, you accepted it not as a human word, but as it actually is, the word of God, which is indeed at work in you who believe.

—1 Thessalonians 2:13

...who have been chosen according to the foreknowledge of God the Father, through the

sanctifying work of the Spirit, to be obedient to Jesus Christ and sprinkled with his blood: Grace and peace be yours in abundance.

—1 Peter 1:2

What does the Holy Spirit do with *your* life?

1. The Holy Spirit is permanently living right inside your body at this very moment! This shows GOD that you belong to Him, body and soul. That means any other spirit that comes along will see that your "house" is already occupied—by the Holy Spirit! Just like when your parents bought their house and showed ownership by moving into it, so the Holy Spirit showed ownership of your body and spirit, by moving in to live in your "house."

   You, however, are not in the realm of the flesh but are in the realm of the Spirit, if indeed the Spirit of God lives in you. And if anyone does not have the Spirit of Christ, they do not belong to Christ.

   —Romans 8:9

   Do you not know that your bodies are temples of the Holy Spirit, who is in you, whom you have received from God? You are not your own.

   —1 Corinthians 6:19

2. The Holy Spirit packages or seals you up, and puts a mailing address on you marked: "Saved. Destination: Heaven—Guaranteed!" Once that is done, no one can tamper with us! It is certainly better and far more reliable than sending a package via the post office!

Now it is God who makes both us and you stand firm in Christ. He anointed us, set his seal of ownership on us, and put his Spirit in our hearts as a deposit, guaranteeing what is to come.

—2 Corinthians 1:21-22

And you also were included in Christ when you heard the message of truth, the gospel of your salvation. When you believed, you were marked in him with a seal, the promised Holy Spirit, who is a deposit guaranteeing our inheritance until the redemption of those who are God's possession—to the praise of his glory.

—Ephesians 1:13-14

And do not grieve the Holy Spirit of God, with whom you were sealed for the day of redemption.

—Ephesians 4:30

3. The Holy Spirit will give you all the ability and power that you need each and every time you go out to live a Christlike life, and especially when you are going out to do some job for GOD. He makes you brave, gives you energy, gives you ideas, etc.

Brothers and sisters, choose seven men from among you who are known to be full of the Spirit and wisdom. We will turn this responsibility over to them.

—Acts 6:3

Then Saul, who was also called Paul, filled with the Holy Spirit, looked straight at Elymas and said, "You are a child of the devil and an enemy of everything that is right! You are full of all kinds of deceit and trickery. Will you never stop perverting the right ways of the Lord? Now the hand of the Lord is against you. You are going to be blind for a time, not even able to see the light of the sun." Immediately mist and darkness came over him, and he groped about, seeking someone to lead him by the hand. When the proconsul saw what had happened, he believed, for he was amazed at the teaching about the Lord.

—Acts 13:9-12

4. The Holy Spirit makes you into a "clone" of Jesus Christ, by teaching you and disciplining you when needed; by praying with you so that GOD knows what you really want to say to Him; by helping you to know when the Enemy is lying to you, so you can protect yourself from doing the wrong things; by making sure that you behave like a real child of GOD's family—a credit to His name!

    But…"*Clone!*" you exclaim in dismay? Relax! That just means you will look, behave, and think like Jesus Christ—but you will still have your own mind with which to think and make choices.

But the fruit of the Spirit is love, joy, peace, forbearance, kindness, goodness, faithfulness, gentleness and self-control. Against such things there is no law.

—Galatians 5:22-23

…these are the things God has revealed to us by his Spirit. The Spirit searches all things, even the deep things of God.

—1 Corinthians 2:10

...in the same way, the Spirit helps us in our weakness. We do not know what we ought to pray for, but the Spirit himself intercedes for us through wordless groans. And he who searches our hearts knows the mind of the Spirit, because the Spirit intercedes for God's people in accordance with the will of God.

—Romans 8:26-27

But you have an anointing from the Holy One, and all of you know the truth.

—1 John 2:20

As for you, the anointing you received from him remains in you, and you do not need anyone to teach you. But as his anointing teaches you about all things and as that anointing is real, not counterfeit-just as it has taught you, remain in him.

—1 John 2:27

For those who are led by the Spirit of God are the children of God.

—Romans 8:14

The Spirit himself testifies with our spirit that we are God's children.

—Romans 8:16

...so in Christ we, though many, form one body, and each member belongs to all the others. We have different gifts, according to the grace given to each of us. If your gift is prophesying, then prophesy in accordance with your faith; if it is serving, then serve; if it is teaching, then teach; if it is to encourage,

then give encouragement; if it is giving, then give generously; if it is to lead, do it diligently; if it is to show mercy, do it cheerfully.

—Romans 12:5-8

What really counts is that you let the Holy Spirit do His work in you! The "new" you will be astounding! Totally!

CHAPTER 19

THE HOLY SPIRIT AND UNBELIEVERS

Does the Holy Spirit have anything to do with the non-believer? Let's look at some examples of what GOD did for you when you were still an unbeliever.

And, *yes,* He did a lot for you!

1. He enabled you to notice that there is a Jesus.

   But when he, the Spirit of truth, comes, he will guide you into all the truth. He will not speak on his own; he will speak only what he hears, and he will tell you what is yet to come. He will glorify me because it is from me that he will receive what he will make known to you.

   —John 16:13-14

2. He sent people to you to share with you what GOD wanted you to know, convincing you to believe and accept in your heart that Jesus died and had paid for your penalty of death.

   ...because our gospel came to you not simply with words but also with power, with the Holy Spirit and deep conviction. You know how we lived among you for your sake.

   —1 Thessalonians 1:5

3. He made you, and can make all those people who live apart from GOD, really aware of sin, and of how bad sin looks to GOD. This makes you and others realize the extent to which you and they are under the inherited penalty of death for GOD's broken law.

   When he comes, he will prove the world to be in the wrong about sin and righteousness and judgment: about sin, because people do not believe in me; about righteousness, because I am going to the Father, where you can see me no longer; and about judgment, because the prince of this world now stands condemned.

   —John 16:8-11

4. He creates the "new person in Christ" when a person becomes "born again" of the Holy Spirit and is baptized.

   Jesus answered, "Very truly I tell you, no one can enter the kingdom of God unless they are born of water and the Spirit."

   —John 3:5

...he saved us, not because of righteous things we had done, but because of his mercy. He saved us through the washing of rebirth and renewal by the Holy Spirit.
—Titus 3:5

GOD sent His Son Jesus and His Holy Spirit into the world to come to the rescue of all kinds of people... especially the very worst and even the most hateful!

Salvation from death is available to *all*, no exceptions!

CHAPTER 20

THE HOLY SPIRIT IN THE OLD TESTAMENT

"We don't often seem to talk about the Holy Spirit in the Old Testament. Did He do things back then?"

Well, the title "Holy Spirit" may not have been used at that time, but the Spirit was definitely at work! All persons in the Trinity were *always* working together, even if one of them may have been working "behind the scenes." (The terms *Holy Ghost* and *Holy Spirit* refer to the same person of the Trinity.)

Examples of the Holy Spirit at work in the Old Testament include when He was:

1. ACTING with the Father and the Son in creation.

   Now the earth was formless and empty, darkness was over the surface of the deep, and the Spirit of God was hovering over the waters.
   —Genesis 1:2 (emphasis mine)

2. GIVING the leaders of Israel and His prophets the ability and the power to do work for GOD.

The LORD said to Moses: "Bring me seventy of Israel's elders who are known to you as leaders and officials among the people. Have them come to the tent of meeting, that they may stand there with you. I will come down and speak with you there, and I will take some of the power of the Spirit that is on you and put it on them. They will share the burden of the people with you so that you will not have to carry it alone."
—Numbers 11:16-17 (emphasis mine)

3. RENEWING creation.

When you send your Spirit, they are created, and you renew the face of the ground.
—Psalm 104:30 (emphasis mine)

4. INDWELLING (or entering) into the minds of Israel's kings to help them perform their kingly duties.

So Samuel took the horn of oil and anointed him in the presence of his brothers, and from that day on the Spirit of the LORD came powerfully upon David. Samuel then went to Ramah.
—1 Samuel 16:13 (emphasis mine)

(This is the same thing that happens when we accept Christ: the Holy Spirit comes inside us and joins with our spirit so that we can do work for God.)

5. INSPIRING (or entering into) the minds of the prophets of Israel and the men who would write out all the words of the Bible.

Concerning this salvation, the prophets, who spoke of the grace that was to come to you, searched intently and with the greatest care, trying to find out the time and circumstances to which the Spirit of Christ in them was pointing when he predicted the sufferings of the Messiah and the glories that would follow.
— 1 Peter 1:10-11 (emphasis mine)

(GOD did this to make sure that what was in the Bible was what He wanted, to let mankind know exactly who GOD is, and how He wants us to live!)

6. 6. LIVES IN THE HEART of every believer in Christ, to motivate each believer to learn about GOD and to do what He wants.

"You stiff-necked people! Your hearts and ears are still uncircumcised. You are just like your ancestors: You always resist the Holy Spirit!"
— Acts 7:51

(GOD's Spirit actually completely joins with our spirit inside our bodies, so that we can know God inside out, and be able to serve GOD. But, as this verse warns, we must not resist what the Holy Spirit instructs us to do.)

In other words, GOD's Holy Spirit gives us His super powers to do GOD's work!

WAY COOL! Our own real, live Superhero!

CHAPTER 21

GRIEVING THE HOLY SPIRIT

We can "grieve" the Holy Spirit and, at the same time, do harm to our own spirits.

As we discovered, without the working of the Holy Spirit in our lives, we would be empty spiritual shells! Without His fruits, we have no satisfying emotions or happiness. But did you know that it is possible to harm our new, born-again spiritual bodies? When we sin after we have accepted Christ, did you know that sin blocks the Holy Spirit in us?

Have you ever had a much beloved grandparent or relative die? Do you remember how you felt at the time? Well, do you also know that every time you choose to disobey GOD, you have made the Holy Spirit feel that same kind of great sadness, and that stops His working in you?

You can grieve the Holy Spirit through:

1. DISOBEDIENCE

   Ephesians 4:30 says, *"And do not grieve the Holy Spirit of God, with whom you were sealed for the day of redemption."* (This is when you decide to do something, knowing all the while that it isn't the right thing to do, and you go ahead and do it anyways!)

2. LYING to Him

   Acts 5:3 says, *"Then Peter said, 'Ananias, how is it that Satan has so filled your heart that you have lied to the Holy Spirit and have kept for yourself some of the money you received for the land?'"* (That is like every time that you pretend to yourself that your sin is "not a real sin," but "just a white lie," in hopes that you can do it without feeling so guilty.)

3. QUENCHING Him with your poor attitudes.

   1 Thessalonians 5:19 says, *"Do not quench the Spirit."* (This is when you extinguish His flame of light in your heart with your grumblings, your constant desire for more "things," your bad treatment of siblings or parents, your neglect of Him, etc.)

4. RESISTING Him.

   Acts 7:51 says, *"You stiff-necked people! Your hearts and ears are still uncircumcised. You are just like your ancestors: You always resist the Holy Spirit!"* (Have you ever heard that little voice inside you saying to be nice to your sibling, and instead you decided or chose to be nasty? Well, that was the Holy Spirit's voice you pushed away so you could choose your own way instead! You resisted the Holy Spirit!)

5. INSULTING Him.

Hebrews 10:29 says, *"How much more severely do you think someone deserves to be punished who has trampled the Son of God underfoot, who has treated as an unholy thing the blood of the covenant that sanctified them, and who has insulted the Spirit of grace?"*

How often have you "put aside" being a Christian (turned away or rejected the Holy Spirit "temporarily") so you could do what you wanted, and then turned back to Him when you felt like it? In other words, have you "used" the Holy Spirit like you would a favorite toy: cuddling it when you feel like it, and then throwing it into a corner?

Any of the above-listed items causes your "spiritual armor" to get large holes—holes that will allow Satan to do great spiritual harm to you.

So how is your relationship with the Holy Spirit? Is that relationship a close one?

[Note: always have your Bible beside you when you read this, so that you can read directly from GOD's Word what He wants you to know. It is the living Word of GOD that can change your heart.]

SECTION 4

JESUS, OUR LORD AND SAVIOUR

CHAPTER 22

JESUS IS GOD

The Bible states that Jesus is God, one of the three persons of the Trinity: *"In the beginning was the Word, and the Word was with God, and the Word was God"* (John 1:1).

Jesus has characteristics that only GOD would have:

1. He is eternal (or lives forever, is without end).

   "I tell you the truth," Jesus answered, "before Abraham was born, I am!"
                                                    —John 8:58

2. He is omnipresent (is everywhere at the same time).

   "For where two or three come together in my name, there am I with them."
                                                    —Matthew 18:20

   He has omniscience (total knowledge of everything).

   "Now we can see that you know all things and that you do not even need to have anyone ask you questions. This makes us believe that you came from God."

—John 16:30

3. He has omnipotence (total power).

"I am the Alpha and the Omega," says the Lord God, "who is, and who was, and who is to come, the Almighty."

—Revelation 1:8

4. He has immutability (never ever changes).

You will roll them up like a robe; like a garment they will be changed. But you remain the same, and your years will never end.

—Hebrews 1:12

Jesus does what only GOD can do:

1. He has authority to forgive sins

But that you may know that the Son of Man has authority on earth to forgive sins.

—Mark 2:10

2. He can give life (can make alive anyone He wants to).

For just as the Father raises the dead and gives them life, even so the Son gives life to whom he is pleased to give it.

—John 5:21

3. He can raise the dead (can make dead people alive again).

"For my Father's will is that everyone who looks to the Son and believes in him shall have eternal life, and I will raise him up at the last day."

—John 6:40

4. He is the final Judge (He makes judgements and carries them out).

Moreover, the Father judges no one, but has entrusted all judgment to the Son...And he has given him authority to judge because he is the Son of Man.

—John 5:22, 27

5. Jesus was given the titles only GOD could have:

"The virgin will conceive and give birth to a son, and they will call him Immanuel" (which means "God with us").

—Matthew 1:23

For to us a child is born, to us a son is given, and the government will be on his shoulders. And he will be called Wonderful Counselor, Mighty God, Everlasting Father, Prince of Peace.

—Isaiah 9:6

On his robe and on his thigh he has this name written:
KING OF KINGS AND LORD OF LORDS.

—Revelation 19:16

...The high priest said to him, "I charge you under oath by the living God: Tell us if you are the Christ, the Son of God."

"You have said so," Jesus replied. "But I say to all of you: From now on you will see the Son of Man sitting at the right hand of the Mighty One and coming on the clouds of heaven."

—Matthew 26:63b-64

"I and the Father are one."

... "We are not stoning you for any of these," replied the Jews, "but for blasphemy, because you, a mere man, claim to be God."

—John 10:30, 33

Because Jesus is GOD, we must worship Him.
Because Jesus is our King, our lives belong to Him.
Because Jesus is our Lord, we must live to serve Him.

CHAPTER 23

JESUS AND THE TRINITY

Jesus is part of the Trinity, and the Three are also One.

JESUS IS CALLED GOD, FATHER, AND COUNSELOR.

> *...to us a child is born, to us a son is given, and the government will be on his shoulders. And he will be called Wonderful Counselor, Mighty God, Everlasting Father, Prince of Peace.*
>
> —Isaiah 9:6

[Note: Here it distinctly shows us that Jesus is one being with the Counselor (who is the Holy Spirit), and that Jesus is one with GOD, and that Jesus is one with the Father.]

JESUS AND HOLY SPIRIT: When Jesus went to heaven and sent the Holy Spirit, it was His own Spirit that He sent. (See Isaiah 9:6 above, where Jesus is called "counselor.")

But the Counselor, the Holy Spirit, whom the Father will send in my name, will teach you all things and will remind you of everything I have said to you.

—John 14:26

JESUS AND GOD ARE BOTH THE MIGHTY GOD.

For to us a child is born, to us a son is given, and the government will be on his shoulders. And he will be called Wonderful Counselor, Mighty God, Everlasting Father, Prince of Peace.

—Isaiah 9:6

"But from now on, the Son of Man will be seated at the right hand of the mighty God."

—Luke 22:69

The Mighty One, God, the LORD, speaks and summons the earth from the rising of the sun to the place where it sets.

—Psalm 50:1

We shouldn't get too hung up on the fact that Jesus is called a Son. For Jesus, the word "Son" describes a far deeper and closer relationship to the Father than we are familiar with in our daily lives.

Jesus came forth from the Father, and is one with the Father. If we consider GOD to be a unique spiritual Being, and an offspring (exactly like the original) is reproduced from the essence of that unique original Being, then the offspring is also called GOD, because He has *all* the characteristics and essence of the original. The reason that the original Being is called Father, and the offspring is called Son, is that the latter came forth from the former.

The unique thing about GOD is that, because GOD is a unique Spirit Being, communication between the Father and the Son is total and unhindered, and because they share the exact same characteristics and essence, they never disagree. Because we are not spiritual beings, we cannot know how they can be three and yet one. But being perfect, all-powerful GOD and Creator, GOD can do anything.

As for the Holy Spirit, He is the person of GOD that carries out what GOD actively sets out to do. In coordination with God the Father and God the Son, God the Holy Spirit carries out all their works on earth. The Holy Spirit also does much of His work through obedient believers.

The purpose for GOD sending forth the Son from the Father was to carry out the work of redeeming mankind from sin and death, and to pay the price demanded by a GOD who not only manifests ultimate love, but is also a just and righteous GOD. (To say GOD is only a GOD of love and not one of justice and righteousness, is to say He is an incomplete and imperfect GOD.)

After Jesus went back to Heaven, He sent the Holy Spirit to minister the believers and to help bring GOD's plan of salvation and redemption of mankind to completion. Thus, in the Trinity, we cannot "separate" the Father, the Son, or the Holy Spirit. They share every single characteristic that GOD has, and because they are spirit, they also are in total agreement and accord with one another. Because they are GOD, they can be Three, and One, at the same time. Wonderful, huh?

John 1:1 says, *"In the beginning was the Word, and the Word was with God, and the Word was God. He was with God in the beginning."*

John 1:14 says, *"The Word became flesh and made his dwelling among us. We have seen his glory, the glory of the One and Only, who came from the Father, full of grace and truth."*

John 1:18 says, *"No one has ever seen God, but God the One and Only, who is at the Father's side, has made him known."*

1 Timothy 3:16 says, *"And without controversy great is the mystery of godliness: God was manifest in the flesh, justified in the Spirit, seen of angels, preached unto the Gentiles, believed on in the world, received up into glory."* (Since there are no other living gods except GOD, godliness can only describe GOD.)

1 Timothy 2:5 says, *"For there is one God and one mediator between God and men, the man Christ Jesus..."*

Titus 2:13-14 says, *"While we wait for the blessed hope—the glorious appearing of our great God and Savior, Jesus Christ, who gave himself for us to redeem us from all wickedness and to purify for himself a people that are his very own, eager to do what is good."*

Hebrews 1:3-4 says, *"The Son is the radiance of God's glory and the exact representation of his being, sustaining all things by his powerful word. After he had provided purification for sins, he sat down at the right hand of the Majesty in heaven. So he became as much superior to the angels as the name he has inherited is superior to theirs."*

Hebrews 1:8 says, *"But about the Son he says, 'Your throne, O God, will last for ever and ever, and righteousness will be the scepter of your kingdom.'"*

THE HOLY SPIRIT AND JESUS' SPIRIT AND GOD'S SPIRIT ARE ONE AND THE SAME SPIRIT.

Romans 8:9 says, *"You, however, are controlled not by the sinful nature but by the Spirit, if the Spirit of God lives in you. And if anyone does not have the Spirit of Christ, he does not belong to Christ."*

1 Corinthians 6:19 says, *"Do you not know that your body is a temple of the Holy Spirit, who is in you, whom you have received from God? You are not your own."*

Galatians 4:6 says, *"Because you are sons, God sent the Spirit of his Son into our hearts, the Spirit who calls out, 'Abba, Father.'"*

Ephesians 3:16-17a says, *"I pray that out of his glorious riches he may strengthen you with power through his Spirit in your inner being, so that Christ may dwell in your hearts through faith..."*

1 Peter 1:11 says, *"...trying to find out the time and circumstances to which the Spirit of Christ in them*

was pointing when he predicted the sufferings of Christ and the glories that would follow."

Romans 8:10 says, *"But if Christ is in you, then even though your body is subject to death because of sin, the Spirit gives life because of righteousness."*

1 Corinthians 12:3 says, *"Therefore I tell you that no one who is speaking by the Spirit of God says, 'Jesus be cursed' and no one can say, 'Jesus is Lord' except by the Holy Spirit."*

Ephesians 4:30 says, *"And do not grieve the Holy Spirit of God, with whom you were sealed for the day of redemption."*

1 Thessalonians 4:8 says, *"Therefore, he who rejects this instruction does not reject man but God, who gives you his Holy Spirit."*

Go to www.biblegateway.com and the NIV version for words to the verses below:

Ephesians 3:4-6; 1 John 3:22-23; 1 Corinthians 6:11.

If you have no Bible, do get one, or download a Bible app onto your cell phone.

CHAPTER 24

THE GOD JESUS WAS ALSO HUMAN

Since Jesus is God, how do we know that He really became a human being when He lived on earth?

1. His mother was a human woman.

   But when the set time had fully come, God sent his Son, born of a woman, born under the law.
   —Galatians 4:4

2. He grew up physically and mentally.

   And the child grew and became strong; he was filled with wisdom, and the grace of God was on him... And Jesus grew in wisdom and stature, and in favor with God and man.
   —Luke 2:40, 52

3. He could get tired.

   Jacob's well was there, and Jesus, tired as he was from the journey, sat down by the well. It was about noon.
   —John 4:6

4. He would get hungry.

   After fasting forty days and forty nights, he was hungry.
   —Matthew 4:2

5. He cried tears.

   Jesus wept.
   —John 11:35

6. He was tempted.

   Then Jesus was led by the Spirit into the wilderness to be tempted by the devil. After fasting forty days and forty nights, he was hungry. The tempter came to him and said, "If you are the Son of God, tell these stones to become bread."
   —Matthew 4:1-3

   Because he himself suffered when he was tempted, he is able to help those who are being tempted.
   —Hebrews 2:18

7. He could get angry and feel very distressed.

   He looked around at them in anger and, deeply distressed at their stubborn hearts, said to the man,

"Stretch out your hand." He stretched it out, and his hand was completely restored.
—Mark 3:5

8. He felt sorry for other people's troubles.

    When he saw the crowds, he had compassion on them, because they were harassed and helpless, like sheep without a shepherd.
    —Matthew 9:36

9. He felt agony (a deep hurt in His soul).

    And being in anguish, he prayed more earnestly, and his sweat was like drops of blood falling to the ground.
    —Luke 22:44

Because Jesus felt and went through everything we do as humans, He really knows our deepest needs, desires, hurts, and *all* we go through in life as no one else can—even those people who love us. He truly understands what we give up in order to follow Him.

Jesus is our ultimate best friend—perfect in every way! He never ever lets us down. He is totally reliable and trustworthy!

CHAPTER 25

OUR WATER FROM HEAVEN

Deuteronomy 33:28b says, *"His heavens shall drop down dew."* (Water rains down from heaven, from GOD, to give physical life. In just the same way, GOD sends down a spiritual water to give us spiritual life.)

Genesis 2:4-5 says, *"This is the account of the heavens and the earth when they were created. When the LORD God made the earth and the heavens, now no shrub of the field had yet appeared on the earth and no plant of the field had yet sprung up, for the LORD God had not sent rain on the earth and there was no one to work the ground."*

Isn't it amazing how all the life in this world of ours is dependent on water? Just think: what would be left if there was *no water*? Think of all the plants and animals: can you think of any of them that can stay alive without water?

So we can see that all physical creatures and organisms rely on water to exist! We could say, in that case, that *water is life!*

Often, we read that Jesus is considered to be the living water, that He is one who can and will give our spirits refreshing rejuvenation.

John 4:14 says, *"...but whoever drinks the water I give him will never thirst. Indeed, the water I give him will become in him a spring of water welling up to eternal life."*

That is exactly what Jesus does. He refreshes and sustains us when we read the Word of God, the Bible. He also does this when He sends the Holy Spirit to live inside our bodies and our human spirits. In just the same way that *water* will nourish our physical bodies and keep everything "running properly," the *Holy Spirit* nourishes our spirits and keeps our spirits strong and healthy. In fact, the Holy Spirit can make our bodies and spirit so healthy that we can eventually become as Adam was—he would have been able to live forever before the curse of death came.

Eternal life for us will happen when Jesus returns for His Bride, the Church, when we will be caught up in the air and changed in the twinkling of an eye (see 1 Corinthians 15:50-54 and Matthew 25).

Allow the Holy Spirit to rejuvenate you! Remember that GOD always works as the Father, the Son, and the Holy Spirit. GOD makes use of the special abilities that each Person of the Trinity has, and yet the Trinity (1 + 1 + 1 = 1) is always together, working together and never working separately.

CHAPTER 26

WHO IS JESUS TO US?

Who is Jesus Christ?

Jesus is GOD's Word. In the incarnation, GOD's own Word took on human form and became flesh. But just as your words are from you, GOD's Word (Jesus) comes from Him.

> John 1:1 says, *"In the beginning was the Word, and the Word was with God, and the Word was God."*

(Do look up *incarnation* in a dictionary.)

Jesus came as a God/Man so that we could each know GOD, the Father, personally.

> John 1:14 says, *"The Word became flesh and made his dwelling among us. We have seen his glory, the glory of the one and only Son, who came from the Father, full of grace and truth."*

Jesus came to get rid of the death caused by our sins. He paid the penalty price for us, so that we could be with GOD forever. He died for you and me.

Now if we died with Christ, we believe that we will also live with him. For we know that since Christ was raised from the dead, he cannot die again; death no longer has mastery over him. The death he died, he died to sin once for all; but the life he lives, he lives to God.

—Romans 6:8-10

1. Jesus is our SAVIOUR. He saved us from eternal separation from GOD.

Salvation is found in no one else, for there is no other name under heaven given to mankind by which we must be saved.

—Acts 4:12

Jesus sacrificed His human life to give us eternal life.

2. Jesus is our LIFE.

Jesus answered, "I am the way and the truth and the life. No one comes to the Father except through me."
—John 14:6

3. Jesus is our LORD.

If you declare with your mouth, "Jesus is Lord" and believe in your heart that God raised him from the dead, you will be saved.

—Romans 10:9

Jesus deserves all our worship and respect. What part of you should Jesus be Lord of? Your time?...your love?...your

money?...your best possessions?...your friendships?...
your goals?...your dreams?...your family?

Think hard...exactly which parts of your life is Jesus
Lord of at this very minute? Is He only Lord of your life at
church on Sundays?

To make some changes, write out a short, doable list
of things that you need to make Jesus the Lord of in your
life, and then *decide* to do them!

Check back in a couple of weeks to see if you have
changed.

CHAPTER 27

THE IMPORTANCE OF JESUS' RESURRECTION

How is it important to us that Jesus rose from the dead and became alive again?

1. Because of Jesus' resurrection from the dead, GOD showed us that Jesus is really GOD's own Son.

   Romans 1:4 says, *"...and who through the Spirit of holiness was appointed the Son of God in power by his resurrection from the dead: Jesus Christ our Lord."*

2. GOD also showed us that He would allow Christ's death on the cross to be the *payment* for all our sins. He would not require any more payment than that for all the sins of mankind.

   Romans 4:25 says, *"He was delivered over to death for our sins and was raised to life for our justification."*

   When Jesus rose from the dead, He actually *overpowered death*, and made it so that we would not have to die any more (we can now live forever if we really believe that Jesus did that for us).

Romans 8:11 says, *"And if the Spirit of him who raised Jesus from the dead is living in you, he who raised Christ from the dead will also give life to your mortal bodies because of his Spirit who lives in you."*

3. GOD tells us in His Word that if we believe that Jesus died and rose from the dead for us, we too can someday die and rise from the dead just like Jesus did. In other words, *death will no longer threaten us*, because we will not stay dead, we will become alive again! We will have resurrection bodies when Christ returns!

1 Corinthians 15:20-21 says, *"But Christ has indeed been raised from the dead, the first fruits of those who have fallen asleep. For since death came through a man, the resurrection of the dead comes also through a man."*

Just think what our new resurrection bodies will be like! Our new bodies may be just like that of Jesus! What neat things we will be able to do!

CHAPTER 28

WHY DID JESUS
HAVE TO SUFFER?

Back when Jesus died, nailing a man to a cross of wood and leaving him to hang there screaming in pain and agony was thought to be the most humiliating and awful way a man could be punished for a serious crime—and of course, the criminal usually died a horrible death!

When GOD sent His Son Jesus to pay for our sins, He chose the *worst* punishment imaginable so that we would know how *bad* He thinks our sins are. GOD wanted us to know how angry He felt at our sinful behavior against Him. Yet, He loved us, too! Or else why would He have sacrificed the life of His only Son for us? Death was ultimate payment for ultimate sin.

He is the atoning sacrifice for our sins, and not only for ours but also for the sins of the whole world.
—1 John 2:2

The high standing of Jesus, as GOD's own Son, sinless and free of sin, made the payment of His Life something that was able to satisfy GOD as legal satisfaction for the sins of *billions* of men, women, and children.

No other person (or angel) could have paid the price for that many people! One or two maybe…but not billions!

Surely he took up our pain and bore our suffering, yet we considered him punished by God, stricken by him, and afflicted. But he was pierced for our transgressions, he was crushed for our iniquities; the punishment that brought us peace was on him, and by his wounds we are healed.
—Isaiah 53:4-5

Otherwise Christ would have had to suffer many times since the creation of the world. But he has appeared once for all at the culmination of the ages to do away with sin by the sacrifice of himself.
—Hebrews 9:26

Only Jesus' payment could satisfy GOD's laws and justice. Only Jesus' sacrifice could bring us GOD's forgiveness.

For he has rescued us from the dominion of darkness and brought us into the kingdom of the Son he loves, in whom we have redemption, the forgiveness of sins.
—Colossians 1:13-14

There is no way you could ever hope to pay Jesus back for what he did for you! He is even going to share His inheritance with you. Because of Him, you are going to be treated like the adopted child of a King!

So, how can you show your love and gratitude to God for what He has done for you? Read this verse below and find out what you can do:

Therefore, I urge you, brothers and sisters, in view of God's mercy, to offer your bodies as a living sacrifice, holy and pleasing to God—this is your true and proper worship. Do not conform to the pattern of this world, but be transformed by the renewing of your mind. Then you will be able to test and approve what God's will is—his good, pleasing and perfect will.
—Romans 12:1-2

We need to love, trust, and obey our GOD, because through Jesus, the Son, GOD showed His extreme love for us.

CHAPTER 29

WHERE IS JESUS NOW?

Where is Jesus now?

(Note: the words "Church," "Bride," and "saints" each describe all the believers in Christ.)

They say Jesus is alive! So where is He?

1. Preparing a place for us in Heaven.

"Do not let your hearts be troubled. You believe in God; believe also in me. My Father's house has many rooms; if that were not so, would I have told you that I am going there to prepare a place for you? And if I go and prepare a place for you, I will come back and take you to be with me that you also may be where I am."

—John 14:1-3

2. Making us acceptable before God.

   Who then is the one who condemns? No one. Christ Jesus who died—more than that, who was raised to life—is at the right hand of God and is also interceding for us.

   —Romans 8:34

3. Looking after us.

   Therefore, since we have a great high priest who has ascended into heaven. Jesus the Son of God, let us hold firmly to the faith we profess.

   —Hebrews 4:14

4. Leading the church on earth.

   And he is the head of the body, the church; he is the beginning and the firstborn from among the dead, so that in everything he might have the supremacy.

   —Colossians 1:18

5. Preparing for His return to earth.

   Jesus is in Heaven, preparing for us and preparing for His return.

   Way back in New Testament times, about two thousand years ago, Jesus Christ went up to heaven forty days after He rose from the dead (the resurrection). In heaven, Jesus was given the place of highest honor. He has reminded us that upon His return, things will happen.

   Therefore this is what the LORD says: "I will return to Jerusalem with mercy, and there my house will be rebuilt. And the measuring line will be stretched out over Jerusalem," declares the LORD Almighty.

—Zechariah 1:16

After this I will return and rebuild David's fallen tent. Its ruins I will rebuild, and I will restore it...

—Acts 15:16

For "you were like sheep going astray," but now you have returned to the Shepherd and Overseer of your souls.

—1 Peter 2:25

(You have turned back to GOD.)

But while they were on their way to buy the oil, the bridegroom arrived. The virgins who were ready went in with him to the wedding banquet. And the door was shut.

—Matthew 25:10

(Jesus, our Bridegroom, will return for His Bride in a way that is described in Matthew 25, the parable of the ten virgins, which warns us to be ready and "in Christ.")

Jesus will stay in heaven until He returns for us, His Bride, the Church. During this first return, it is only necessary that we believers see Jesus, as we will go to His Father's house up in Heaven for our wedding to Jesus and our marriage feast! An invisible return, just for us!

For the Lord himself will come down from heaven, with a loud command, with the voice of the archangel and with the trumpet call of God, and the dead in Christ will rise first. After that, we who are still alive and are left will be caught up together with them in the clouds to meet the Lord in the air. And so we will be with the Lord forever. Therefore encourage one another with these words.

—1 Thessalonians 4:16-18

Then I heard what sounded like a great multitude, like the roar of rushing waters and like loud peals of thunder, shouting: "Hallelujah! For our Lord God Almighty reigns. Let us rejoice and be glad and give him glory! For the wedding of the Lamb has come, and his bride has made herself ready. Fine linen, bright and clean, was given her to wear." (Fine linen stands for the righteous acts of God's holy people.) Then the angel said to me, "Write this: Blessed are those who are invited to the wedding supper of the Lamb!" And he added, "These are the true words of God."

—Revelation 19:6-9 (emphasis mine)

When All People See Christ Return

When Jesus returns visibly to earth, He will return with His Church, His Bride. At that time, everyone left on earth (all those who had rejected Jesus) will see Him descending on the clouds, accompanied by the Church, His Bride, as He had promised.

Matthew 26:64 says, *"You have said so," Jesus replied. "But I say to all of you: From now on you will see the Son of Man sitting at the right hand of the Mighty*

One and coming on the clouds of heaven" (emphasis mine).

Revelation 19:14 says, *"The armies of heaven were following him, riding on white horses and dressed in fine linen, white and clean" (emphasis mine). ("Fine linen" refers to the Bride, the Church, as in the parable of the ten virgins.)*

Revelation 19:7-8a says, *"Let us rejoice and be glad and give him glory! For the wedding of the Lamb has come, and his bride has made herself ready. Fine linen, bright and clean, was given her to wear"* (emphasis mine).

So we know that we believers, who are the Bride of Christ, will return with Christ when He reveals Himself visibly to all the people on earth who had rejected Him.

Returning as the King of kings, Jesus will show His power as King. He will have Satan locked up so he can do nothing for a while.

And I saw an angel coming down out of heaven, having the key to the Abyss and holding in his hand a great chain. He seized the dragon, that ancient serpent, who is the devil, or Satan, and bound him for a thousand years. He threw him into the Abyss, and locked and sealed it over him, to keep him from deceiving the nations anymore until the thousand years were ended. After that, he must be set free for a short time.

—Revelation 20:1-3

Then, for one thousand years, Jesus and those of His Church who have died for Him (they are called "martyrs") will rule the earth and all the people.

> *I saw thrones on which were seated those who had been given authority to judge. And I saw the souls of those who had been beheaded because of their testimony about Jesus and because of the word of God. They had not worshipped the beast or its image and had not received its mark on their foreheads or their hands. They came to life and reigned with Christ a thousand years.*
>
> —Revelation 20:4

The Judging of Those Still Alive

After the one thousand years have ended, Satan will be released from prison and allowed to go out into the earth and try to get people to follow him. Then he and his evil army of followers will gather to fight Jesus and His saints in what is called the Battle of Armageddon. GOD will then destroy Satan and his followers!

Luke 21:20 says, *"When you see Jerusalem being surrounded by armies, you will know that its desolation is near."*

(Also read Revelation 20:7-10 in your Bible to find out how Jesus will deal with Satan and his followers when Jesus returns.)

The Judging of Those Who Have Died

Finally, as the King of kings, Jesus will judge every person who ever lived on earth, including all people who have died. Unbelievers, too, will be resurrected and then punished for their sins—those who have *not* taken Jesus up on His offer to take their punishment for them. And others, like you and other believers who have accepted Jesus, will be ushered into Heaven to eternal life with GOD.

(Read Matthew 25:31-46 in your Bible. Like the parable of the ten virgins, this last section of the chapter is a warning to us from Jesus, to stick closely to GOD's Word, so we will be ready when Jesus returns for us.)

And I saw the dead, great and small, standing before the throne, and books were opened. Another book was opened, which is the book of life. The dead were judged according to what they had done as recorded in the books...each person was judged according to what they had done. Then death and Hades were thrown into the lake of fire. The lake of fire is the second death. Anyone whose name was not found written in the book of life was thrown into the lake of fire.

—Revelation 20:12, 13b-15

Punishment is severe for rejecting GOD!

SECTION 5

THE LIFE
WE MUST LIVE

CHAPTER 30

FACING A HOLY GOD

Can we really face GOD...right now?

How is it, that just because we have accepted Christ as Saviour, we can now stand before a Holy GOD? Aren't we still sinful? Wouldn't we be struck dead in His presence?

Well, yes, we would be struck dead...*if* we were to come before GOD on our own. But we are coming with Jesus' Holy Spirit within us! So when we come before GOD, He looks at us and sees Jesus, and Jesus' sinlessness. He does not see our sinfulness. We are *righteous*, and therefore *right* before GOD. We have GOD's DNA.

> *Therefore, since we have been justified through faith, we have peace with God through our Lord Jesus Christ, through whom we have gained access by faith into this grace in which we now stand. And we rejoice in the hope of the glory of God.*
> —Romans 5:1-2

Imagine that! All we had to do was to *believe* (that's another word for *have faith*) in Jesus. Just think of all the suffering that Jesus had to go through so we could happily face GOD and not feel ashamed and guilty, covered in filthy sins.

We were full of sin and had absolutely *no* right to see GOD, yet GOD loved us and wanted to help us be with Him again.

> *For God so loved the world that he gave his one and only Son, that whoever believes in him shall not perish but have eternal life.*
>
> — John 3:16

By covering ourselves with Jesus' sinlessness, GOD is able to regard us as legally sinless, and we are able to enter into heaven to be with Him. That is called *justification*, a term which means *satisfying the law of GOD*. This is done through Jesus. Because of Jesus, we are made right, made "okay" in GOD's eyes—even though we ourselves really are not.

Each of us can personally accept that Jesus died for us, and made us holy before GOD! Why? Because that first broken law was satisfied in a legal, just way, and because Jesus took the punishment or penalty for us. So, even if we were to stand in front of GOD the Judge right at this very moment, we would not owe payment, like a life sentence in a horrible prison or the death penalty. We will not come under GOD's judgment, and all because of Jesus!

CHAPTER 31

GOD CHOSE US

"Divine Election." This phrase means *GOD chooses*. He does the choosing regarding who actually gets saved in the end. He has the right to do so, and He has sole authority about who ends up as His child, living with Him in Heaven for all eternity. He has this right because He is our Maker and Creator!

Suppose we were a ceramic pot, made by the Potter. If we turned out to be imperfect, the Potter would have the right to smush us up (like clay) and start again, right? In other words, because GOD made us, He has the right to do what He wishes with us. We are very fortunate to have a GOD who loves us, imperfect as we are!

For he chose us in him before the creation of the world to be holy and blameless in his sight. In love he predestined us to be adopted as his sons through Jesus Christ, in accordance with his pleasure and will...
—Ephesians 1:4-5

As our Creator, GOD is able to rule everything in accordance with His will. But, happily, GOD had great plans for us—and He has had them since before He created us!

> *For those God foreknew he also predestined to be conformed to the image of his Son, that he might be the firstborn among many brothers and sisters. And those he predestined, he also called; those he called, he also justified; those he justified, he also glorified.*
>
> —Romans 8:29-30

> *...he predestined us for adoption to sonship through Jesus Christ, in accordance with his pleasure and will...*
>
> —Ephesians 1:5

So how come we still have the right of "choice"? How are we able to choose to accept Christ, if GOD has already chosen who will be saved? Isn't that a contradiction? It sounds that way, but you'll see it is *not* a contradiction if you take into account that GOD has *always* known the past, present, and future of all mankind, including you and me. He knew you before you were born, and He knew what choices you would make, and so He already knew whether you were salvageable when He decided to choose you. He made an informed decision! After all, He is an ultra-intelligent GOD!

Now just because GOD has made His informed choice does not mean He has taken away your right to choose. After all, *you* didn't know ahead of time how things would turn out! You just went ahead and made your own personal decision to accept Christ as your Saviour and Lord, because you wanted to! But GOD knew that you would end up wanting to do His Will and please Him!

Ahh! The mysteries of our great and wonderful GOD and Saviour! *So mind-boggling!*

CHAPTER 32

BELIEVERS IN AN UNBELIEVING WORLD

So how do we get along in the world now? According to GOD's Word, we are to obey the manmade laws of the countries in which we live.

Slaves, obey your earthly masters with respect and fear, and with sincerity of heart, just as you would obey Christ. Obey them not only to win their favor when their eye is on you, but as slaves of Christ, doing the will of God from your heart. Serve wholeheartedly, as if you were serving the Lord, not people, because you know that the Lord will reward each one for whatever good they do, whether they are slave or free.
　　　　　　　　　　　　　　　　—Ephesians 6:5-8

"Show me the coin used for paying the tax." They brought him a denarius, and he asked them, "Whose image is this? And whose inscription?"

"Caesar's," they replied.

Then he said to them, "So give back to Caesar what is Caesar's, and to God what is God's."
—Matthew 22:19-21

But we are not to do anything that goes against GOD in any way. GOD is our ultimate authority. There could possibly come a time when human law requires us to do something that is against what GOD requires of us. In such a situation, we are to do as GOD instructs in His Word. Yes, the Word of GOD gives us specific instructions as to how we are to live while on Earth. We answer to GOD above all!

A good example of this is the behavior of Daniel and his friends as recounted in the Old Testament of the Bible! Remember the story you learned in Sunday School about Daniel in the lion's den? Daniel had prayed to his GOD for help when jealous men in Persia plotted to get rid of him. Because Daniel chose to always obey and trust in his GOD, his enemies could not successfully harm him!

"Daniel, servant of the living God, has your God, whom you serve continually, been able to rescue you from the lions?"

Daniel answered, "May the king live forever! My God sent his angel, and he shut the mouths of the lions. They have not hurt me, because I was found innocent in his sight."
—Daniel 6:20b-22a

The lesson here is that GOD can protect us if we always follow GOD when faced with choosing between GOD's demands and man's demands! On top of that, we can even endure suffering when it comes, because we know that we will end up in heaven with GOD.

CHAPTER 33

WE ARE DISCIPLES OF
JESUS CHRIST

Let's talk about being a disciple of Jesus—about being a disciple of GOD's kingdom.

Jesus promised us that He would send the Holy Spirit to indwell us. He promised this to *all* His disciples.

> *But the Counselor, the Holy Spirit, whom the Father will send in my name, will teach you all things and will remind you of everything I have said to you*
> —John 14:26

So if you have the Holy Spirit indwelling you, does that make you a good disciple of Jesus? Well, that depends on what exactly a *disciple* is, doesn't it?

A *disciple* is a person that has chosen to accept Jesus Christ as the leader of his/her life, and committed to studying His teachings and following His commands by obeying them and by telling others about Him.

To accept Jesus as your Leader, you would do the same things as you would when you are a citizen in a country, or the subject of a King.

You would...

1. First, say the prayer to accept Jesus as your Saviour and Lord (much like saying the Pledge of Allegiance, promising to submit to by loyal to the United States).

2. Next, also in that prayer, you promise to turn your life over to Jesus, and to live your life according to Jesus' teachings. (This is like acknowledging that your daily actions will be judged under the laws of the country, and promising to live as a law-abiding citizen.)

3. Study the Bible to find out all that you can about what Jesus requires of you as His disciple. (This is just like what you would do for your Prime Minister or Queen, in your new country or kingdom, by reading history books, books on their laws, and books that tell you the rules of living in your new country/kingdom, so that you can be a good citizen, a credit to your country!)

4. When you meet people who do not know Jesus, you enthusiastically *tell* them all about Jesus, because He commands you to do so. (This would be like going and telling other people about the wonderful benefits of living in your home country, so that they, too, can live the good life!)

Therefore go and make disciples of all nations, baptizing them in the name of the Father and of the Son and of the Holy Spirit, and teaching them to obey

everything I have commanded you. And surely I am
with you always, to the very end of the age.
—Matthew 28:19-20

REMEMBER:

... you cannot obey Jesus' Great Commission, and baptize others if you don't know Jesus as your Saviour.

... you cannot teach others if you don't know Jesus' life story, His teachings, and His commands.

Once you have accepted Christ, and after you have studied the Word (trying always to obey the Word in your life), *then* you can go out in obedience to Jesus' command to spread the good news about salvation to other people. All this will be accomplished by the Holy Spirit in you!

CHAPTER 34

IN CHRIST ONLY

Charles Spurgeon, in his sermonette "The Marvellous Magnet," gives us strong encouragement to not be discouraged and not be afraid of telling others about Jesus. He says to "try the preaching of a crucified, risen, and ascended Savior." In other words, we must depend on the work and life of Jesus to attract people to GOD. Preaching a social gospel where we try to address the ills of this world is not what we are called to do; preaching Jesus and His death on the cross is what GOD requires of us as obedient believers.

> *And if Christ has not been raised, our preaching is useless and so is your faith.*
> —1 Corinthians 15:14

We should not be like those Hollywood movies where sensational entertainment and fancy graphics are required to make "hits" and to attract large, paying audiences. When telling our friends and acquaintances about GOD's gift of salvation, we are *not* to rely on our own resources, but on those of the Holy Spirit in us.

No song and dance, no complicated theatrics, just the plain truth from GOD's Word. The truth about the gospel will activate the workings of the Holy Spirit. Imagine this conversation with your friend. You ask, "What is the greatest fear you will ever have?" "Death!" your friend replies. You say, "Did you know that death actually came to mankind because of sin against GOD?"

> *...but you must not eat from the tree of the knowledge of good and evil, for when you eat from it you will certainly die.*
>
> *—Genesis 2:17*

> *And the* Lord *God said, "The man has now become like one of us, knowing good and evil. He must not be allowed to reach out his hand and take also from the tree of life and eat, and live forever."*
>
> *—Genesis 3:22*

Tell your friend, "You can stop feeling that great, overwhelming fear, because GOD, who created all things, sent His Son, Jesus, to die on the cross. And when Jesus did that, He *defeated death* by rising from the dead. And, as the Son of GOD, He is now seated in a position of great power in heaven."

> *Death has been swallowed up in victory.*
>
> *—1 Corinthians 15:54b*

> *...he will swallow up death forever. The Sovereign* Lord *will wipe away the tears from all faces; he will*

remove his people's disgrace from all the earth. The
LORD has spoken. In that day they will say, "Surely
this is our God; we trusted in him, and he saved us.
This is the LORD, we trusted in him; let us rejoice and
be glad in his salvation."

—Isaiah 25:8-9

You tell your friend, "To defeat death, just as Jesus did,
all you need to do is to accept that Jesus died for you and
your sins. Ask Jesus to save you! Choose to turn your life
back to GOD, and GOD will allow you to become a real
part of His family."

Repent, then, and turn to God, so that your sins may
be wiped out, that times of refreshing may come from
the Lord...

—Acts 3:19

And everyone who calls on the name of the LORD
will be saved; for on Mount Zion and in Jerusalem
there will be deliverance, as the LORD has said, even
among the survivors whom the LORD calls.

—Joel 2:32

For the Son of Man came to seek and to save what
was lost.

—Luke 19:10

"You will be a brother or sister of Jesus, the Son of
GOD. You will be given a share in Jesus' inheritance! What
wealth, what riches are waiting for those who belong to
GOD's family!"

Praise be to the God and Father of our Lord Jesus Christ! In his great mercy he has given us new birth into a living hope through the resurrection of Jesus Christ from the dead, and into an inheritance that can never perish, spoil or fade. This inheritance is kept in heaven for you...

—1 Peter 1:3-4

You can have an inheritance that will never disappear, spoil, or fade, and it is kept waiting in heaven just for you!

CHAPTER 35

It's Hard to Be Christlike

Are you finding it hard to act like a Christian *all* of the time? Often as Christians, we wonder why "nothing" is coming out from our *being* Christians. Why can't we love our siblings, and always share our possessions? If we are so full of love, why aren't we doing "Christian" things, like serving GOD? Why can't we, even when we try?

The second letter of Peter sheds some light on this dilemma of ours:

> *For this very reason, make every effort to add to your faith goodness; and to goodness, knowledge; and to knowledge, self-control; and to self-control, perseverance; and to perseverance, godliness; and to godliness, mutual affection; and to mutual affection, love. For if you possess these qualities in increasing measure, they will keep you from being ineffective and unproductive in your knowledge of our Lord Jesus Christ.*
>
> —2 Peter 1:5-8

At times, we may even endure suffering from unbelievers, because we are Christians; God allows us to experience suffering to mature and develop our characters.

> *Not only so, but we also glory in our sufferings, because we know that suffering produces perseverance; perseverance, character; and character, hope…*
> —Romans 5:3-4

Dr. Charles H. Spurgeon, a respected biblical theologian, showed that for us Christians to be fruitful, "we must have certain things come into us; for nothing can come out of us which is not first of all within us." These things come from the Holy Spirit.

We need to have…

1. FAITH (accept Jesus as Saviour),
2. VIRTUE (decide to stop sinning),
3. KNOWLEDGE (learn, from the Bible and the Holy Spirit in us, how God wants us to live),
4. TEMPERANCE (hold back negative feelings),
5. PATIENCE (do not get impatient when others behave badly),
6. GODLINESS (practice the fruits of the Holy Spirit, as found in Galatians 5:22-23), and,
7. BROTHERLY LOVE (love others more than yourself).

"Wow!" you might say. "That's impossible! It really is! I can't do that! *No way* can I be loving and Christlike all the time! That is more than I can do…more than I can be!"

But wait, GOD knows what you and I are like. *That* is why He is giving us the Holy Spirit to help us. The best thing about this is that GOD's Holy Spirit can change us from the inside out, so that we can naturally behave as a Christian should. The Holy Spirit comes to live in you when you repent and accept Jesus as your Saviour.

And when you get baptized, that is when the Holy Spirit officially starts to prepare you to serve GOD. Then He prepares you to become a Sunday School teacher, a pastor, a deacon, an elder, or some other type of servant of GOD.

The Holy Spirit will begin by filling you with all the necessary spiritual qualities (see the list above). All these qualities must be filled to overflowing in us, so that we behave in a Christlike manner to other people one hundred percent of the time. (This will show that we are filled with the Holy Spirit). Then, and only then, will we be able to serve GOD and be real, authentic, godly Christians.

Pray daily and ask GOD to give you the above qualities. Because He also wants those qualities to be in you, He *will* give you those desires of your heart!

CHAPTER 36

OUR GOD IS SO COOL!

How does it make you feel, to know that your GOD is the "coolest of the cool" in the whole universe? Your loving Father is the richest and the most powerful, and He can do absolutely *anything* He wants! And *you* are His child!

Even when something really bad is happening to us, we know that in the end things will be all right. GOD says...

> Not only so, but we also glory in our sufferings, because we know that suffering produces perseverance; perseverance, character; and character, hope.
>
> —Romans 5:3-4

> Consider it pure joy, my brothers and sisters, whenever you face trials of many kinds, because you know that the testing of your faith produces perseverance. Let perseverance finish its work so that you may be mature and complete, not lacking anything.
>
> —James 1:2-4

We can even be joyful when facing death, because GOD promises us that..

And we know that in all things God works for the good of those who love him, who have been called according to his purpose. For those God foreknew he also predestined to be conformed to the image of his Son, that he might be the firstborn among many brothers and sisters.

—Romans 8:28-29

Therefore we do not lose heart. Though outwardly we are wasting away, yet inwardly we are being renewed day by day. For our light and momentary troubles are achieving for us an eternal glory that far outweighs them all. So we fix our eyes not on what is seen, but on what is unseen, since what is seen is temporary, but what is unseen is eternal.

—2 Corinthians 4:16-18

For we know that if the earthly tent we live in is destroyed, we have a building from God, an eternal house in heaven, not built by human hands. Meanwhile we groan, longing to be clothed instead with our heavenly dwelling, because when we are clothed, we will not be found naked. For while we are in this tent, we groan and are burdened, because we do not wish to be unclothed but to be clothed instead with our heavenly dwelling, so that what is mortal may be swallowed up by life. Now the one who has fashioned us for this very purpose is God, who has given us the Spirit as a deposit, guaranteeing what is to come. Therefore we are always confident and know that as long as we are at home in the body we are away from the Lord. For we live by faith, not by sight. We are confident, I say, and would prefer to be away from the body and at home with the Lord. So we make it our goal to please him, whether we are at home in the body or away from it.

—2 Corinthians 5:1-9

All of this means that you really need to remember to thank GOD for *all* He gives you. Do you realize that GOD could just as easily have caused you to be born in other, less fortunate parts of the world, where kids wearing filthy rags live in constant fear of dying, and never lose the gnawing hunger in their stomachs?

Look around you, right this minute...thank GOD out loud for everything you see, because those are *your* blessings from GOD, who loves *you*!

CHAPTER 37

OUR INHERITANCE IN CHRIST

Sit down for a moment, right now, and consider this. A real, all-powerful King, an actual GOD, the only one in existence, has offered to adopt you into His family! How wonderful is that? Better by far than winning the multimillion-dollar power-ball lottery! And we are talking about a love that is big time! For good! Something that will never run out! Money runs out, right? But GOD's offer is for eternity. If you accept, you are set forever!

Do you hope to inherit something from your parents? From your conception and birth, you inherited DNA: fifty percent from your mother, fifty percent from your father. But suppose you could have your DNA changed into GOD's DNA? That would mean you are an actual offspring of GOD! How does *that* work?

Well, accept GOD's gift of salvation and adoption, and GOD's Holy Spirit will enter you to make the necessary changes to your DNA! It is possible because GOD is your Creator and can do those adjustments. But GOD will not make such major changes until you give permission by choosing to accept His offer!

After acceptance, you are possessed by GOD's Holy Spirit, who works in you to bring Jesus fully into you. That is accomplished by your reading of the Bible, the Word (Jesus is the Living Word), and putting what you learn into action in your life. A real change in your behavior and thoughts will show that you really are becoming like Jesus, internally. That makes you a true child of GOD!

As GOD's child (through spiritual DNA adoption), you also have inherited the same abilities that Jesus has inherited. (Read Ephesians 1:5, for more on our adoption by GOD.) Remember what Jesus was able to do? Increase a meal of seven loaves and two fishes, so that 5,000 hungry people could be fed!

> *And he directed the people to sit down on the grass. Taking the five loaves and the two fish and looking up to heaven, he gave thanks and broke the loaves. Then he gave them to the disciples, and the disciples gave them to the people.*
>
> —Matthew 14:19

How about the wedding where Jesus turned barrels of water into a rich, flavorful wine for the guests? (Read the full chapter of John 2 about the wedding Jesus attended at Cana in Galilee.) Or how about when Jesus healed a blind man, who then received back his sight?

> *As he went along, he saw a man blind from birth. His disciples asked him, "Rabbi, who sinned, this man or his parents, that he was born blind?"*

"Neither this man nor his parents sinned," said Jesus, "but this happened so that the works of God might be displayed in him."

—John 9:1-3 (I recommend you read the full chapter)

Those are just some of the benefits of belonging to the family of GOD. It was GOD's great love for us that caused Him to offer such a grand gift to save us from death and to reestablish our relationship with Him—a relationship broken through the disobedience of our ancestors, Adam and Eve.

GOD created mankind with many, many fine benefits. But those were basically thrown away when the first man and woman chose to break GOD's first law. To inherit what is actually a royal godly inheritance is more than you or I could ever deserve, based on our actual selves as descendants of Adam and Eve. The love of our GOD is what saves us from an eternity separated from Him!

So, a very grand inheritance is what we can look forward to as GOD's adopted children, and the alternative is far too terrible to contemplate!

CHAPTER 38

SHARING THE GOSPEL

Why do we need to tell others about what Jesus did for us? Because He told us to! He wants us to share the gospel, to tell about how He has saved us all from the consequences of our sins, and to tell about the other things connected with reestablishing a good relationship with GOD.

> *Then Jesus came to them and said, "All authority in heaven and on earth has been given to me. Therefore go and make disciples of all nations, baptizing them in the name of the Father and of the Son and of the Holy Spirit, and teaching them to obey everything I have commanded you. And surely I am with you always, to the very end of the age."*
> —Matthew 28:18-20

How do we share and what do we say? Perhaps we can learn from Dr. Peter Golin, an Elder at Willingdon Church in Burnaby, British Columbia, Canada (elders@ willingdon.org).

Below are notes from a workshop attended by the author, given by Dr. Peter Golin.

As a very simple and effective way to present the gospel, the drawing of an outline of a cross can visually show the important elements that comprise the gospel in its entirety.

The main seven elements of the gospel are: *creation, sin, the cross, resurrection, only by faith, repentance,* and *surrender.*

To visually imprint the elements in our mind, imagine an outlined drawing of a cross. On the upper part of the left arm is *creation*, at the top is *sin*, on the upper part of the right arm is *cross*, and next, on the lower part of the left arm, is *resurrection*. In the middle is *only by faith*, on the lower part of the right arm is *repentance*, and lastly, at the bottom, is *surrender*.

We must always start with prayers to GOD first, on behalf of the person whom you want to be saved.

Prayer brings GOD into the equation, for it is only He who saves, and only His Holy Spirit who can convict a sinful heart. Only after prayer can we look for an opportune time in which to actually share the gospel with someone.

The order of this presentation clearly sets out the complete gospel through which GOD purposes to save each person who chooses, through faith, to trust and obey Him.

An acronym for remembering the gospel elements is: CCRROSS: Creation, Cross, Resurrection, Repentance, Only by Faith, Sin, Surrender.

Here is the orderly presentation of the gospel to the unbeliever:

1. Creation: You are special to GOD, made for His joyful pleasure.
2. Sin: You have been actively living without GOD in your life, and this is a grievous sin against GOD.
3. Cross: Jesus came to reunite you with GOD, and to pay for your personal disobedience by dying on the cross for you.
4. Resurrection: Like Jesus, you will be resurrected, you will be a new creation, free of the sins which had separated you from GOD.
5. Only by Faith: You chose to believe GOD's Word, which says believing the gospel will reestablish your relationship with GOD.
6. Repentance: You now consciously put GOD first, turning from your old ways and putting them behind you. You decide to learn from His Word and follow His ways.
7. Surrender: Instead of living for your own self-gratification, now you resolve to live for GOD, recognizing His sovereign right over you and your life and always resolving to obey Him and His rules.

Once your friend has believed, follow up by giving them a Bible, introducing them to a Bible-believing church, and helping them join a supportive group of Christians for regular fellowship.

Be available to answer questions and give support as they grow in Christ. Pray for spiritual protection and continued growth for the new believer.

GOD's Christmas Salvation Message

God created us, we broke God's first law, and we became cursed with death.

> *…but you must not eat from the tree of the knowledge of good and evil, for when you eat from it you will certainly die.*
>
> *—Genesis 2:17*

> *Then the man and his wife heard the sound of the Lord God as he was walking in the garden in the cool of the day, and they hid from the Lord God among the trees of the garden. But the Lord God called to the man, "Where are you?"*

> *He answered, "I heard you in the garden, and I was afraid because I was naked; so I hid."*

And he said, "Who told you that you were naked? Have you eaten from the tree that I commanded you not to eat from?"

The man said, "The woman you put here with me—she gave me some fruit from the tree, and I ate it."

Then the LORD God said to the woman, "What is this you have done?"

The woman said, "The serpent deceived me, and I ate."

So the LORD God said to the serpent, "Because you have done this,

"Cursed are you above all livestock and all wild animals! You will crawl on your belly and you will eat dust all the days of your life. And I will put enmity between you and the woman, and between your offspring and hers; he will crush your head, and you will strike his heel."

To the woman he said, "I will make your pains in childbearing very severe; with painful labor you will give birth to children. Your desire will be for your husband, and he will rule over you."

To Adam he said, "Because you listened to your wife and ate fruit from the tree about which I commanded you, 'You must not eat from it,'

"Cursed is the ground because of you; through painful toil you will eat food from it all the days of your life. It will produce thorns and thistles for you, and you *will eat the plants of the field. By the sweat of your brow, you will eat your food until you return to the ground, since from it you were taken; for dust you are and to dust you will return."*

—Genesis 3:8-19

GOD came as the Word to us to fix our *problem of death.*

Therefore, just as sin entered the world through one man, and death through sin, and in this way death came to all people, because all sinned...

—Romans 5:12

But God demonstrates his own love for us in this: While we were still sinners, Christ died for us.

—Romans 5:8

In fact, the law requires that nearly everything be cleansed with blood, and without the shedding of blood there is no forgiveness.

—Hebrews 9:22

The next day John saw Jesus coming toward him and said, "Look, the Lamb of God, who takes away the sin of the world!"

—John 1:29

Therefore the Lord himself will give you a sign: The virgin will conceive and give birth to a son, and will call him Immanuel.

—Isaiah 7:14

"The virgin will conceive and give birth to a son, and they will call him Immanuel" (which means "God with us").

—Matthew 1:23

In the beginning was the Word, and the Word was with God, and the Word was God.

—John 1:1

GOD came to us as a human being, Jesus Christ, the Word of GOD.

Beyond all question, the mystery from which true godliness springs is great: He appeared in the flesh, was vindicated by the Spirit, was seen by angels, was preached among the nations, was believed on in the world, was taken up in glory.

—1 Timothy 3:16

This is how the birth of Jesus the Messiah came about: His mother Mary was pledged to be married to Joseph, but before they came together, she was found to be pregnant through the Holy Spirit. Because Joseph her husband was faithful to the law, and yet did not want to expose her to public disgrace, he had in mind to divorce her quietly.

But after he had considered this, an angel of the Lord appeared to him in a dream and said, "Joseph son of David, do not be afraid to take Mary home as your wife, because what is conceived in her is from the Holy Spirit. She will give birth to a son, and you are to give him the name Jesus, because he will save his people from their sins."

All this took place to fulfill what the Lord had said through the prophet: "The virgin will conceive and give birth to a son, and they will call him Immanuel" *(which means "God with us").*

When Joseph woke up, he did what the angel of the Lord had commanded him and took Mary home as his wife. But he did not consummate their marriage until she gave birth to a son. And he gave him the name Jesus.

—Matthew 1:18-25

GOD gives us only one of two choices: to remain under our death sentence or *to accept life through Jesus Christ.*

For God so loved the world that he gave his one and only Son, that whoever believes in him shall not perish but have eternal life.

—John 3:16

We all must make our own individual choice verbally before GOD.

...how shall we escape if we ignore so great a salvation? This salvation, which was first announced by the Lord, was confirmed to us by those who heard him.

—Hebrews 2:3

...for all have sinned and fall short of the glory of God...

—Romans 3:23

...to open their eyes and turn them from darkness to light, and from the power of Satan to God, so that they may receive forgiveness of sins and a place among those who are sanctified by faith in me.

—Acts 26:18

Pray to GOD, who wants to reestablish a relationship with you. (To *repent* means *to turn away*; "sins" means the curse of death we all have.)

But I pray to you, LORD, in the time of your favor; in your great love, O God, answer me with your sure salvation.

—Psalm 69:13

Peter replied, "Repent and be baptized, every one of you, in the name of Jesus Christ for the forgiveness of your sins. And you will receive the gift of the Holy Spirit."

—Acts 2:38

Therefore, my friends, I want you to know that through Jesus the forgiveness of sins is proclaimed to you.

—Acts 13:38

I have declared to both Jews and Greeks that they must turn to God in repentance and have faith in our Lord Jesus.

—Acts 20:21

Do you want salvation from death? Pray and let GOD know. Find a quiet place where you are alone. Face upwards towards heaven, and say these words aloud: *"God, I want your free gift of salvation from death. I ask for forgiveness for all my sins, and I chose to turn away from my sins, and accept that Jesus died on the cross to pay for my sins. I give my life to you, God, as Lord over me and to be my Saviour. Amen."*

You, now, need not live in fear of death. Did you know that, though Christians do die physically, there will be a second death? It comes after Jesus Christ returns to earth, as He promised He would. At that time, all will be resurrected to face judgment by Jesus. Those who rejected Christ will be condemned to the second death, and those who accepted Christ will go to heaven to live forever with GOD. At the first death, Christians sleep (read 1 Corinthians 15:6, 20).

> *Who then is the one who condemns? No one. Christ Jesus who died—more than that, who was raised to life—is at the right hand of God and is also interceding for us.*
>
> —Romans 8:34

Unbelievers are resurrected for judgment and will experience a second death, a spiritual death. They will for all eternity be separated from GOD, and all His blessings of love, and all good things. That is what hell is all about: total separation from GOD, a nightmare with no end.

BIBLIOGRAPHY

Note to readers: the author has read many Christian books, and watched and listened to many sermons. Thus, much of what was read and listened to may have remained in her mind. If you, the reader, should find that ideas presented are ones you originally thought up, or are yours only, please do let the author know, so proper credit can be assigned to the proper people.

1. Vision TV Canada. Gospel to Go #1-2: *Naomi Shriemers TV Testimony Episode.* Friday, January 15, 2016. TV, Shaw Channel 10. TV broadcast.
2. Dr. Charles Stanley. *"The Loneliness of Drinking from the Old Well,"* sermon. One of two thirty-minute episodes on TV Shaw Channel 10 from 8 to 9 a.m. Sunday, April 3, 2016. www.intouch.org. Video.
3. www.biblegateway.com. Source of *verses* from the NIV New International Version of the Bible. Online, print.
4. NIV New International Version of the Bible. Source of *verses quoted* by the author. Online, print.
5. Stetzer, Ed. *What is the Gospel?*. https://www.christianitytoday.com/edstetzer/2015/june/what-is-gospel.html.

6. Slick, Matt. *What is the real gospel message?* https://carm.org/oneness-pentecostal/what-is-the-real-gospel-message/.

7. Google: World Book Discover. *Definition of mercy.* https://worldbookonline.com/wbdiscover/home.

8. Google: Bible Timelines. *Definition of grace.* https://www.bibletimelines.com/timelines.

9. Golin, Dr. Peter. *Living the Gospel: How to Share Your Faith in Jesus Christ Without Fear.* 290 pages. http://www.ctministries.info/the-book/. Print, paperback.

10. Spurgeon, Dr. Charles H. *The Marvellous Magnet.* No. 1717-29:229. A Sermon Delivered On Lord's Day Evening, March 11, 1883, By C. H. Spurgeon, At The Metropolitan Tabernacle, Newington. https://answersingenesis.org/education/spurgeon-sermons/1717-the-marvellous-magnet/.

REFERENCES

1. Barnhouse, Donald Grey. *Romans, 2 Volumes.* Pages not specified. EERDMANS, Hendrickson Publishers Marketing. LLC. www.christian- book.com. C1952, c1953, c1954, c1959. Second Printing. December 2014. Print, paperback.
2. Hodge, Charles. *Systematic Theology, 3 Volumes.* 2260 pages. HENDRICKSON PUBLISHERS. 2013. Print, hardcover.
3. Gurnall, William. *The Christian in Complete Armour. 3 Volumes.* 1036 pages. Updated. Originally written in 1655. BANNER OF TRUTH. Print, paperback.
4. Our Daily Bread Ministries of Canada, multiple authors. *The Daily Bread.* Quarterly daily devotional publication.
5. Copeland, Kenneth. *Believer's Voice of Victory episodes.* https://www.kcm.org/watch/live. TV broadcast on Sundays. Shaw Channel 10, at 10 to 10:30 a.m. TV, thirty-minute videos.
6. Dollar, Creflo. *Creflo Dollar Ministries.* https://www. creflodollarministries.org/. Shaw Channel 10, every Sunday at 10:30 to 11 a.m. Thirty-minute episodes. Thirty-minute video format.

7. Jeremiah, Dr. David. *Turning Point.* TV episodes. Broadcast on Shaw Channel 10, on Sundays at 9:30 to 10 a.m. Thirty-minute episodes.

8. Spurgeon, Dr. Charles H. *Spurgeon's Sermons, 5 Volumes.* Hendrickson Publishers. 4328 pages. Hardcover.

9. Posted by Reyes, Frances. Youtube.com: *Gabriel Fernandes' online videos.* An online prayer ministry by Gabriel Fernandes.

10. Piper, John. *What is the Christian Gospel?* http://www.desiringgod.org/articles/what-is-the-christian-gospel.

11. Cutting Edge. *How do I Know I am Saved?* http://www.cuttingedge.org/news/salvation.html.

12. www.christianbook.com. Source of some reference *books bought and read by the author.*

13. www.amazon.ca. Source of some *reference books* bought and read by the author.

CPSIA information can be obtained
at www.ICGtesting.com
Printed in the USA
LVHW021423131122
733035LV00023B/465